THE FIGHTING COCK

Also by JEAN ANOUILH

Natasha Perry and Rex Harrison
Act Two

THE
FIGHTING COCK

Jean Anouilh

Adapted by LUCIENNE HILL

New York COWARD-McCANN, Inc.

© 1960 by Jean Anouilh and Lucienne Hill

Library of Congress Catalog
Number: 60-9669

MANUFACTURED IN THE UNITED STATES OF AMERICA

The Fighting Cock
opened in New York
December 8, 1959,
at the Anta
Theatre with
the following
cast:

CHARACTERS
(In order of appearance)

THE GENERAL	*Rex Harrison*
THE DOCTOR	*Geoffrey Lumb*
TOTO, *the General's son*	*Claude Gersene*
MARIE-CHRISTINE, *the General's daughter*	*Judy Sanford*
THE MILKMAN'S SON	*Rhoden Streeter*
THE MILKMAN	*Roger De Koven*
FATHER GREGORY	*Michael Gough*
SOPHIE, *the General's daughter*	*Margo Anders*
TARQUIN EDWARD MENDIGALES	*Roddy McDowall*
BISE, *the General's sister*	*Jane Lillig*
AGLAE, *the General's wife*	*Natasha Perry*
LEDELLUC	*Arthur Treacher*
MICHEPAIN	*Gerald Hiken*
BARON HENRI BELAZOR	*Alan MacNaughtan*

The Fighting Cock was produced by
                    Kermit Bloomgarden Productions, Inc.
Directed by Peter Brook
Settings and costumes by Rolf Gerard

TIME: The Present Day
PLACE: A Country House in France

ACT ONE

The General's Study
Scene I: Late Afternoon
Scene II: The Same Evening

ACT TWO

The Garden
A Few Days Later. Afternoon

ACT ONE

SCENE ONE

ACT ONE

SCENE ONE

The GENERAL'S *study. The* DOCTOR *is busy taking the* GENERAL'S *temperature.*

GENERAL. What was I talking about?

DOCTOR. Your military career.

GENERAL. Right! Where was I?

DOCTOR. May 1940. The German breakthrough.

GENERAL. Ah, yes. The German breakthrough. May 1940. In command of an armored battalion in the very center of the gap. The enemy flooding in on both flanks and in the rear. All contacts with Headquarters broken. Suddenly I remember the immortal words of Marshal Foch.

> *Quoting.*
"My left has crumbled, my right is shattered, my rear is in ruins, I attack." I never did think much of Foch as a strategist. His immortal words led me straight to a German prison

camp. Escaped a year later and got out of Germany disguised as a Dominican monk and got back to France just in time to join in the third plot to do away with old Marshal Pétain. It failed. Back in prison—escaped again—got to England in a fishing boat.

DOCTOR. In what disguise this time?

GENERAL. A fisherman, of course. Went to Free French Headquarters in London and the following day was deposited in North Africa by parachute to organize the plot to hand over the French Navy to the Allies. It succeeded. I was forthwith promoted to General. On Liberation Day, 1945, I entered Paris at the head of my brigade.

DOCTOR. Oh, yes, I remember seeing you in the newsreels.

GENERAL. There I was at the age of 38, a great hero—if you will excuse the term, Doctor—of a republic that stood for everything I despised. I looked around me at the people in office and they were the same slimy, corrupt incompetents who had led to the collapse of France. I joined another plot to replace them with men of honor. A week later back in prison again. This time they packed me off to Pontsegur, down in the Pyrenees.

DOCTOR. Did you escape this time?

GENERAL. I considered it. But you know, conditions for escaping in peacetime aren't quite the same as they are in war. To begin with, where the devil do you escape to? No. I decided to stay. It's a fine building, Pontsegur. Beautifully designed in the 14th century and vastly improved in the 17th—from the point of view of defense, that is, not comfort. I nearly froze to death. One regulation blanket, exercises in the yard in six inches of snow, cold showers at ten below zero—the whole medieval routine. It takes more than that to break me.

DOCTOR. Roll up your sleeve, will you?

GENERAL. I survive six months in their icy dungeons and the day I leave I catch a filthy cold. Four months to get myself fighting fit again, at the end of which I learn that I've been sacked. The youngest general in France and the youngest to be pensioned off. I held every record! My career was complete. So, fourteen years ago, I retire down here, meet a girl considerably younger than myself, marry her, start raising cabbages, make some children—but that's a temporary occupation. After a while, the idle life begins to tell on me. I decide to write my memoirs . . . like all generals. I put the title at the top of the page. Chapter I. I lay down my pen for a second in order to think . . . (a piece of folly generals never commit as a rule) . . . and I realize that I have absolutely nothing to say. I tell you, Doctor, for a second everything went black. The pit of despair yawned at my feet and there I stood, gaping like a great baboon. Was that my life?

DOCTOR. Steady!

GENERAL. And then, quite by chance, one morning—I'll tell you how in a moment—I stumble on the maggots. I was saved!

DOCTOR. Maggots?

GENERAL. Maggots. Those little things that wriggle. It suddenly struck me that the reason France was in such chaos—had been in fact for years and years—was quite simply this:

there were maggots in the fruit. France was crawling with worms!

DOCTOR. Oh, yes?

GENERAL. And not only France either. The rest of the world as well. Maggoty through and through.

DOCTOR. You know, General, the world may be maggoty, but you're not too sound yourself. Do you realize your blood pressure is up to two hundred? That's very high, you know. Tell me, wasn't my predecessor worried about that?

GENERAL. Not in the least . . . his was 210. "You lucky devil," he used to say, as he shut up his bag, "only 200— why you're just a youngster." Then he'd hand me one of his cigars, I'd fetch my decanter of port and we'd quietly settle back and empty it together.

DOCTOR. A drop! The merest drop! Mine is 210 too.

GENERAL. How splendid! I like you more and more, Doctor.

DOCTOR. Seriously, though, you must take care of yourself.

GENERAL. I'll be frank with you, Doctor. I didn't call you in to discuss my health. There's absolutely nothing wrong with me. It's the world that is sick.

DOCTOR. Yes, but what can we do about it?

GENERAL. I have a plot.

DOCTOR. Oh, no. Not another one.

GENERAL. You're new to the neighborhood, but I'm sure we think alike. I only called you in to get to know you better. I am forming the spearhead of a movement to rid the world of maggots. Are you prepared to join me?

[18

DOCTOR. What, with my list of patients? Up at six, never in bed before midnight. I have precious little time for movements. And what with the odd confinement, like today . . .

GENERAL. The entire world is in labor, Doctor. This great planet, bursting with riches, is writhing in agony and all we do is sit by her bedside concocting ways to cheat the tax authorities.

DOCTOR. Too true.

GENERAL. Cheating is our great obsession! We're all trying to find something to make our lives a little easier, a little more agreeable. Give us a bit more comfort! That's our battle cry now. All the ingenuity of men, which was harnessed for so long to nobility and beauty, is now bent on finding something a bit softer to put under their bottoms. Contraptions to make our drinks cooler, our houses warmer, our beds softer . . .

DOCTOR. And very nice too!

GENERAL. Nice! Nice! It's disgusting! Don't you see where all this has got us? To music without the effort of making it, to sport you sit and watch, to books that nobody bothers to read (they digest them for you—it's easier and it saves time), to ideas without thinking, to money without sweat, to taste without the bother of acquiring it (there are glossy magazines that take care of all that for you). Short cuts to the good life. Cheating—that's our great aim now. I'll tell you, Doctor. It's a maggot's eye view. The worms have brought us round to their wormy ways.

    A knock. He growls.

What is it?

A SHRILL VOICE. Papa!

GENERAL (*shouting*). I said I wasn't to be disturbed! The doctor's sounding my chest!

VOICE. You finished ages ago! I can see you through the keyhole! Papa, I've got to speak to you.

GENERAL. Well, come in.

MARIE-CHRISTINE *comes in with* TOTO.

MARIE-CHRISTINE. Papa! The milkman's son pinched my bottom!

GENERAL. Turn the other cheek. Tell him I'll box his ears.

MARIE-CHRISTINE. I did. He said his father said you were a dirty reactionary.

GENERAL. Tell him to send his father along to me. I'll ram a few good reactions down his throat.

MARIE-CHRISTINE. He said his father was stronger than you.

GENERAL. Which he is. All right you two, run along. I'll look into it. And remember, a good soldier always protects his rear. That's what things have come to, Doctor.

DOCTOR. Steer clear of the milkman, General. He's the local agitator. He's all-powerful on the Town Council. You'll have no end of trouble. Besides he's a brute.

GENERAL. So am I.

DOCTOR. Yes, but you're a skinny brute and he weighs half a ton.

GENERAL. What can he do to me? Knock me down a dozen times? I'll get back on my feet and knock *him* down a dozen times! For I know something he doesn't know. I've eaten Ministafia!

DOCTOR. Ministafia?

GENERAL. Yes. When I was twelve my cousins and I found a wonderful roll of shiny red paper in the attic. We called it Ministafia. Whenever we had anything a bit risky to do—a rock fight against the boys in the nearby village, say—we'd chew a bit of it and suddenly we weren't afraid of a mortal thing. Since they put me on the retired list, I've stuffed myself with Ministafia. I'm ready to advance. I am holding my first secret meeting here at 8 o'clock tonight. Are you with me?

DOCTOR. A meeting, you say? What exactly do you propose to do?

GENERAL. Rid the world of its maggots and teach the people the meaning of honor.

DOCTOR. Honor? Does your movement aim to teach them honor too?

GENERAL. To the best of them. To the rest, I'd like to restore a wondering uneasy yearning for it. It is by their ability to die for something incomprehensible to the vast majority, that a handful of men have succeeded, over the centuries, in winning the respect of the world.

DOCTOR. I would be delighted to come along, General, but I don't really think I'm your man. If you wanted to seize the firehouse, or blow up the Town Hall, I don't say I wouldn't go along with you. After all, things are in such a mess it couldn't do any harm. But it strikes me that your movement is pitting itself against the tide of history, and there, I warn you, you haven't a hope.

GENERAL. The tide of history! Every age has produced bogey

words like that. I defy any historian to tell you what it means. But I'm keeping you, Doctor. You must have half a dozen patients suffering from acute wind, all paid for by socialized medicine. That's progress too, Doctor. The poor man's right to a free belch.

DOCTOR. Yes. But it doubles my working day!

GENERAL. Good! It may teach you your trade! We've had five thousand years of your hit-or-miss methods! I'll see you to your car. Are you getting a new one this year? They've stopped looking like cakes of soap: they're more like suppositories now. Progress marches on!

DOCTOR. What a man! Can you wonder your blood pressure's high?

> *They go out.* MARIE-CHRISTINE *comes in with* TOTO.

MARIE-CHRISTINE. Papa! The milkman's son said—Damn! He's gone!

> *Calling offstage.*

Come in, if you dare!

> *The* MILKMAN'S SON *comes in.*

MILKBOY. I told you, I'm not afraid of your father! Is this his study?

MARIE-CHRISTINE. Yes.

MILKBOY. All those swords up there—are they his?

MARIE-CHRISTINE. Yes.

MILKBOY. Can I touch one?

MARIE-CHRISTINE. If you like.

MILKBOY. What would he say?

MARIE-CHRISTINE. You'll soon find out.

MILKBOY. Ooh, look at that! Are these what he used to kill Arabs with?

MARIE-CHRISTINE. Yes.

MILKBOY. My father says all people are equal—now don't you forget that. Still—if it were Red Indians that must have been terrific! Here, you take this. You be the Indian.

TOTO. Indians!

MILKBOY. They've carried you off, see, the dirty redskins, and I'm coming to rescue you. Come on, you! Fight, you coward. I'm on the warpath!

TOTO. Help! Help!

MILKBOY. I'll teach you to lay your hands on a white woman, you filthy Indian.

> *He yells his warcry and gallops on to the terrified* TOTO. *His charge brings him face to face with the* GENERAL *who has come in again. He stops dead.*

GENERAL. Stand easy!

MILKBOY. Yes, sir!

GENERAL. Who are you?

MILKBOY. The milkman's son, sir.

GENERAL (*To* MILKBOY). What cackhanded halfwit taught you to hold a sword?

MILKBOY. Nobody, sir!

GENERAL. Fine education you've had! Here, like this. Up with it! En garde! I thrust, you parry. I cut, you parry. You cut, I feint. Not bad. Come on, you cut, I parry.

Enter the MILKMAN.

I cut flank, I cut head.

MILKMAN. I might have known it! Reactionary beast! Blood-sucker! Grinder of the faces of the poor! Just you wait. It won't be long now.

Exit MILKMAN *with his son.*

GENERAL. A maggot!

To MARIE-CHRISTINE

Is that the young man who pinches your bottom?

MARIE-CHRISTINE. Yes, Papa.

GENERAL. Not much to boast about, is he? Next time pick one with a broader chest.

MARIE-CHRISTINE *goes out.*

Tell me, Toto, are you afraid of the milkman's boy?

TOTO. Yes.

GENERAL. And when you're frightened, what do you do?

TOTO. I run.

GENERAL. In which direction?

TOTO. Backwards.

GENERAL. Now listen, it's quite simple. Next time you're frightened, don't run backwards, run forwards instead. Backwards or forwards, what difference does it make, pro-vided you run? Only then, you see, he'll be scared instead of you. That's the whole secret. In battle, everybody's frightened. The only difference is which way you run.

TOTO. Suppose he isn't scared?

GENERAL. If you run fast enough you'll scare him all right. Do you know what Ministafia is?

TOTO. No.

GENERAL. I'll give you a piece.

> *He rummages on his desk and finally pulls out a*
> *sheet of red blotting paper.*

I shan't give you a big bit. Ministafia is in short supply
these days. Mustn't waste it. There. That'll do the trick.
It's not such good quality as the pre-war stuff, but it works
just the same. Whenever you feel frightened just munch a
tiny bit of it.

TOTO. And swallow it?

GENERAL. Yes.

TOTO. Mother will say it's dirty.

GENERAL. Women don't know much about things like Ministafia. Best to keep quiet about it.

TOTO. But suppose she says "What have you got in your
mouth?"

GENERAL. Swallow first and then say "Nothing."

TOTO. But that's telling a lie. The last time you explained
about honor you said honor said not to tell lies.

GENERAL. Quite. But when it specially concerns a point of
honor, you make a quick decision and you lie just the same.
Lord alive, how difficult it all is! Make haste and grow up.
I'll explain it to you then. But from now on you're quite
safe with that Ministafia, so just you run away forwards.

> *Enter the* PRIEST.

PRIEST. General, it's five o'clock!

GENERAL. Good afternoon, Father. Run along, my boy. Father Gregory and I have serious parish matters to discuss.

PRIEST (*to* TOTO). Now then, young man, I'll see you tonight with your catechism. And if you aren't word perfect this time, watch out for the seat of your pants!

> TOTO *chews a piece of Ministafia and bravely marches out.*

What's the child eating blotting paper for?

GENERAL. I can't imagine. Now, Father, I'm all yours. I'm afraid I haven't done so well this week. I've been having a little trouble with my verbs.

PRIEST. Let's see, shall we? You really must make an effort, General. Otherwise I shall have to rap you smartly on the knuckles.

GENERAL. *Amare*—to love. *Amo, amas, amat, amomus— amamus, amatis, amant.*
Monere—to rule, to warn. *Moneo, mones, monet, moni- mus—monemus, monetis, monent.*
Audire—to hear. *Audio, audas, audat—audis, audit, audi- mus, auditis, audiunt.*
Regere—to rule. *Rego, regis, regit, regimus, regitis, regess —regunt!*
Does it amuse you to see me act the fool like this?

PRIEST. No, I find it very touching. I wish sometimes that you hadn't sworn me to secrecy. I think it's very brave of you to struggle with Latin at your age. I should so like to quote you as an example.

GENERAL. That's right! And give the neighbors one more reason to laugh at me! Anyway, it's nothing to make a fuss about. I'm only doing my duty. Toto thinks I'm a hero. He is convinced that I can jump ten yards with both feet together. That I can swim like a fish and that I can knock the milkman senseless with a flick of my wrist. For him my virtues form part of the ordered balance of the world. I wasn't going to saddle him with a father who couldn't help him with his homework. But we're playing truant. My son is growing fast and I'll never master Latin before he does. Where were we?

PRIEST. We were about to correct your little piece of prose, if that's all right. "*Ut exit Caesar reviro urbi vestam.*" Do you know how you rendered that?

GENERAL. No.

PRIEST. At the exit, Caesar put on his city suit.

GENERAL. Wasn't that right? It struck me as rather neat.

PRIEST. It's neat, but it isn't right. "*Ut exit Caesar reviro urbi vestam*" is translated as "Then Caesar put on his toga and left the city."

GENERAL (*disappointed*). Mine was nicer.

PRIEST. Possibly. But that is the exact translation.

GENERAL. Ah, Father. I wonder if it isn't a mistake to insist on translating things too accurately.

PRIEST. If you want to learn Latin, it's essential.

SOPHIE *comes bursting in.*

SOPHIE. Papa! Oh, excuse me, Father Gregory, I thought Papa was alone.

GENERAL. How dare you come bursting in like a herd of elephants! I might have been writing my memoirs.

SOPHIE. You know you've never written more than the title. Anyway I looked through the keyhole.

PRIEST. I see that keyholes are much in use in this house.

GENERAL. They are. And to make it more convenient, they've lost the keys. What did you want?

SOPHIE. Papa. Tarquin Edward Mendigales is coming.

GENERAL. Tarquin Edward Mendigales—who's he?

SOPHIE. My fiancé. He just telephoned.

PRIEST. Why, I hadn't heard the glad news! So Mlle. Sophie is engaged to be married!

GENERAL. I've only just heard the glad news myself.

PRIEST (*confused*). Oh, I'm so sorry . . .

GENERAL. Don't apologize. That's a piece of information I receive, without undue astonishment, every three months.

SOPHIE (*hurt*). Papa, that's very unkind! Last summer I may have made a mistake over Urbain Gravelotte—I was very young, you know—and even last winter over Jean-François Piedelievre—I'd only danced with him twice. But Tarquin Edward Mendigales is the love of my life! And he's actually coming to the house!

GENERAL (*defeated*). Well, bring him in.

      SOPHIE *goes*.

PRIEST. Mendigales? It sounds familiar . . . That big new factory that makes plastic tableware—isn't the managing director a certain Melchior Mendigales?

GENERAL (*glumly*). Plastic tableware!

PRIEST (*after a brief hesitation*). General . . . are you not a little worried that Sophie's youthful—and quite understandable—impulsiveness might induce her to . . . er . . .

GENERAL (*with a worried sigh*). Ah, yes, Father, I am indeed. I'm never anything else.

PRIEST. You must be firm, General. You have spoilt young Sophie, you know.

GENERAL. I'll plead guilty to that, for the purposes of argument. But do you really believe upbringing can do much to change a person's nature? Sophie is the very image of her mother.

PRIEST. That was your first wife.

GENERAL. In a manner of speaking, Father—it was only a brief liaison. In the course of an official tour of the Opéra Comique in Casablanca, where I was a captain in the 8th Dragoons. She admitted to twenty-eight but she was really forty-one. At that age, one can hardly say that it was I who spoilt her. Anyway, I shouldn't have had time. Six weeks of passion, spiced with attempts at suicide, all bungled, and then she came to tell me—in tears, I will say that for her —that she had fallen in love with the tenor. A sort of Roman emperor with a face like a Dutch cheese. I suffered like a dog. I even spent an entire night, like a lovesick schoolboy, cleaning my service revolver; and then the company resumed its tour, carrying them away, the tenor and her, and leaving me in my little darkened room, alone with my black sorrow—as the poet says—plus one or two unpaid bills. The ship had scarcely left the harbor when some kind soul came to tell me that during the six weeks when I thought I was singing Tristan to her Isolde, she had been consistently unfaithful to me with the elevator boy at the Grand Hotel.

PRIEST. My poor friend.

29]

GENERAL. A year later, Yasmina (or Minny, to give her the name she was born with) brought me the baby—on the grounds that it interfered with her career—in the course of another tour of the Opéra Comique, in Egypt this time (where I was stationed as military attaché), and I entrusted the fruits of our guilty union (as you might put it, Father) to the Sisters of Mercy in Alexandria. I couldn't have done much better than that, now could I? There's not much they don't know about training the young. Well, you see the result? Sophie is Sophie. How could she be anything else?

SOPHIE. Papa! He's here!
             She runs out again.

PRIEST. I think perhaps I ought to leave you—

GENERAL (*panicking*). No! Don't go! The Army and the Church must stand shoulder to shoulder!
             Re-enter SOPHIE *with a young man.*
Papa, this is Tarquin Edward Mendigales!

GENERAL. Good afternoon.

MENDIGALES. General, I'm very proud to shake you by the hand.

GENERAL. Why?

SOPHIE. Papa! You're not to be disagreeable to Tarquin Edward!

GENERAL (*with blatant insincerity*). I'm not being disagreeable. He says he's proud to shake me by the hand and I ask him why. Just small talk, gracious me! I moved in polite society before you did, my child. Still, if you prefer us to launch into an argument about it, we will. I loathe arguments, but I'm unbeatable. Why are you proud to shake me by the hand, young man?

MENDIGALES. Because you're a great hero of the French Resistance, General.

GENERAL. That's my affair.

MENDIGALES. Pardon me, General, but it concerns us all. We all know what we owe you.

GENERAL. You owe me nothing.

MENDIGALES. Oh, General, that's not true! I don't think you quite realize what an inspiration your war record is to my generation!

GENERAL. I don't consider that the mere luck of being on the winning side is a necessary guarantee of my integrity.

MENDIGALES. Your integrity is beyond question, General.

GENERAL (*quietly*). Integrity is always a fragile thing, young man. I should hate to look like a man who had bet on the right horse. To tell you the truth, I threw in my lot, half out of temper, in a desperate cause. I triumphed. Right. I went back inside my tent. I want no tips.

MENDIGALES. Those are harsh words, General.

GENERAL. So were the events, young man. But on what grounds—apart from the fairly common one of being in love with my daughter—do you presume to discuss such personal matters?

MENDIGALES. You and I have a lot in common, General.

GENERAL. Do we? I should be intrigued to know what, exactly?

MENDIGALES. My father was in the Resistance too, you see.

GENERAL. Indeed?

MENDIGALES. He spent the war, at the risk of his life, manufacturing faulty concrete for the Germans. It was partly thanks to him that the Atlantic Wall collapsed.

GENERAL. Splendid. Congratulate him for me. I did notice, in the Normandy landings, that there were whole stretches you could cut into like butter. He should have pinned up a billboard.

MENDIGALES. As for me, I was too young, I'm afraid. I was only 12. But I always made a point of refusing the vitamin pills they gave us at school. And I listened in to the London broadcasts every night, on a little crystal set I made myself—clandestinely, of course. Even on the occasions when Papa, who was playing a double game, clenched his fists with hatred and entertained German generals at dinner. Those evenings, I must say, it was rather dangerous.

GENERAL. Well, well! You intrepid little fellow. And didn't they give you a medal for it?

MENDIGALES (*oblivious of the irony*). Oh, it was nothing . . .

GENERAL (*tweaking his ear*). Come, come, don't be so modest.

MENDIGALES. Oow!

GENERAL. When it comes to war, nothing's trivial—in retrospect. I know actresses who won the Croix de Guerre for distinguished services in bed!

SOPHIE. Father, you're being utterly hateful! I'll leave home one of these days, you see if I don't! Come along, Tarquin Edward.

[32

MENDIGALES. Sir.

> *He springs briefly to attention and goes out with dignity.*

GENERAL. Endearing specimen, isn't he? A perfect maggot if ever I saw one.

PRIEST. Oh, come, General. He seems a perfectly normal and ordinary young man.

GENERAL. Exactly. That's the distinguishing mark of the maggot. Perfectly normal and ordinary to look at. The roundness, the bloom, the sweet perfection of the fruit matters not one bit to the maggot. All he cares about is digging himself in.

PRIEST (*reproachfully, and with a touch of the professional manner*). My son! Allow me to call you my son . . .

GENERAL. Why not? You'll make me feel young again. I need it.

PRIEST. Why this perpetual desire to shock? Why this need to provoke people, to soil everything, to rake the mud, of which we all know—alas—that our poor human flesh is made? My son—I shall continue to call you my son, despite your sarcasm—why so much bitterness?

GENERAL (*tonelessly and a little embarrassed*). It isn't bitterness, Father. It's pain. For half a century now I've ached with it. It's beginning to get a little tedious. As a small boy, I'd seen it all quite differently. I've never got over that.

PRIEST. But it is quite different, of course—here. We've all had to face that. We must arm ourselves with patience and courage.

33]

GENERAL. Patience I never did have. I can't change my nature. As for courage—well, I try. "Man is an animal, inconsolable and gay." I never could remember who it was who said that, but I take off my hat to him.

> *Abruptly he picks up the red blotting paper from his desk and chews a piece. Then he hands some to the* PRIEST.

Would you like a bit?

PRIEST (*blinking*). A bit of what? Is it edible?

> *He eyes his piece of blotting paper suspiciously.*

GENERAL (*laughing*). Yes. But it's like all hocus-pocus, you have to believe in it. You ought to know, eh, Father.

> *Guffawing to hide his embarrassment.*

Lord, there's bad taste for you! I'm sorry. Take no notice. It's only my fun. That doesn't stop me being very fond of you.

> *He gives him a rough embrace. Enter* BISE. *She stops short and shrieks.*

BISE. Ludovic!

GENERAL (*jumping from force of habit*). What's the matter with you? It's Father Gregory!

> *To the* PRIEST.

You see, the last time, my sister caught me kissing the maid.

> *Hastily.*

All strictly honorable, of course. Otherwise I shouldn't be telling you, Father. The girl had just told me she was expecting a baby.

> *Elucidating further.*

By the butcher, I mean, of course. They called him Ludovic after me. I was the godfather, you know. Anyway the child looked exactly like the butcher. A big nose and lots of red hair—

> *They have gone out.* BISE *is alone in the room. Now we see that she is in tears, her handkerchief crumpled into a ball in her hand. She paces feverishly about the room and finally collapses with a moan onto the couch.*

BISE. I'll never dare to tell! Never! At my time of life!
> *The* GENERAL *comes back.*

GENERAL. Oh Lord! What is it now?

BISE (*sitting up*). Ludovic! You're the only one I can confide in!

GENERAL (*grunting*). I'm afraid you're probably right. What's the matter?

BISE. Ludovic, I think someone is in love with me.

GENERAL. The age of miracles will never cease.

BISE. A man!

GENERAL. That's normal.

BISE. A worthless man.

GENERAL. That's normal too.

BISE. Ludovic, I am irrevocably compromised.

GENERAL. Let's not exaggerate. Nobody is ever irrevocably compromised in France.

BISE. We aren't discussing France! A woman's reputation is a very fragile thing, Ludovic, remember that.

GENERAL. Dammit, you're in credit! Your reputation has been unassailable for forty something years—and unassailed.

BISE. Those happy days are over now.

GENERAL (*starting*). Great God!—What's that?

BISE (*in a whisper*). I've given in.

GENERAL (*struck speechless at first, suddenly bursts out laughing*). I'd call that very good news!
     Pensively.
But who in the world could . . .

BISE. One of your friends, Ludovic. You are my elder brother, my only protector. I insist you summon this man and force him to make amends. Your personal honor is at stake.

GENERAL (*grumbling*). My personal honor! You're putting my honor in some weird places, aren't you?

BISE. Ludovic! You are a foul-minded boor! What have you dared to imagine?

GENERAL (*embarrassed*). Well, I don't know . . . You're screwing your handkerchief into a ball, you're blubbering, you tell me you're compromised, you say you gave in . . . If you're talking in metaphors say so, and tell me in good plain language.

BISE. Christian Lebelluc, that attractive, worthless creature, has taken advantage of me. There. Is that plain enough?

GENERAL (*twinkling*). Lebelluc? You're not serious?

BISE. Your best friend!

GENERAL. Now let's not exaggerate. He's fond of his food and we dine together once a week. However, a man can be fond of his food and still . . . What exactly do you mean by "taking advantage"?

BISE. Ludovic, don't force me to go into details!

GENERAL. Oh, no! I'm not plunging into a whole unlikely drama with my eyes shut. What does your meager brain understand by taking advantage?

BISE. You asked me to speak plainly. Taking advantage are plain words, aren't they?
She looks at him with broken dignity.
Very well. You've asked for it. I'll tell you.
She begins.
Christian Lebelluc had been looking at me for years . . .

GENERAL. When he met you, just like everyone else.

BISE. No. Not like everyone else. There was a glint in his eye.

GENERAL. You dreamed it. It's a trick of the light. Ask any photographer.

BISE (*cutting in*). There is no light, Ludovic, which can produce the gleam of lust.

GENERAL. Lust is rarer than old maids think.

BISE. Anyway, so long as it was only a glint in his eye—which he probably couldn't control—I said nothing about it. Some days ago, he went on to action. Suddenly, one evening, in a doorway, on the all too convenient pretext of letting me go first, his hand touched my waist.

GENERAL (*impatiently*). Well?

BISE. Then, a moment later, in the drawing room, when I handed him a cup of tea, I saw his eyes burning with desire.

GENERAL. He's very fond of tea. Perhaps he was thirsty.

BISE. No. He didn't even drink it.

GENERAL. Perhaps he didn't want tea. Perhaps he'd have preferred brandy.

37]

BISE (*shaking her head*). No, Ludovic. No woman can mistake a look like that. He was thirsty for me.

GENERAL. Did you give him a drink?

> BISE *stands still a moment, shaking with silent indignation. Then she wails.*

BISE. I'll drown myself, Ludovic!

> *She runs out.*

GENERAL (*shouting after her*). Don't drown yourself without giving me the facts! Did you give him a drink?

> No answer. BISE *is no doubt tearing like a demented thing through the garden. He watches her for a second or two and then comes back into the room.*
>
> *Chuckling.*

Poor old Lebelluc! He's started something!

> AGLAE *comes in. She is young, much younger than the* GENERAL, *charming, gentle and withdrawn, with just a touch of hardness under her gentleness. She is carrying an armful of many colored flowers, which she will arrange in a vase during the following scene.*

AGLAE. There you are.

> *At sight of her, the* GENERAL *is transformed. He is suddenly younger, more attentive; his voice grows softer. He goes to her and kisses her hand.*

GENERAL. Were you looking for me, my dove? What pretty flowers you've found. I walked round the garden this morning and I thought to myself—nothing is growing.

AGLAE (*softly as she arranges her flowers*). You don't know how to look.

The GENERAL *has sat down, as if soothed by her presence. He lights a cigar and smokes it contentedly.*

GENERAL. No. It's true, I charge this way and that, blustering, and I don't know how to use my eyes. You said you would cure me of that bad habit, Aglae.

AGLAE (*still gently*). Can one be cured of one's bad habits?

GENERAL. By love, sometimes . . . At least, so they say in books. You should know something about that, eh? You're a great reader.

AGLAE. I'm tired of reading about life from books.

GENERAL. Yet that's where it shows up best.

AGLAE (*in the same smooth tone of voice as she continues to arrange her flowers*). When you married me, you were very concerned about the difference in our ages. Do you remember how I laughed?

GENERAL. Four clear notes that whisked away, as if by magic, every one of my gray hairs, I shall always remember it.

AGLAE. We had just come in from my father's garden, where you told me you loved me. And I was arranging a vase of flowers in the dark drawing room, just like today. I burst out laughing, your fears were so silly and so unfounded, and I told you that I loved you too. I have never stopped loving you since that day, Ludovic, and thinking you were young.

GENERAL. Even when the gray hairs came back to the attack?

AGLAE. Your face had something a little rough about it. They have given it charm. Let's not pursue this discussion, it

39]

hasn't any meaning. It's not because my husband is a little older than myself that I am bored.

GENERAL. Are you bored?

AGLAE (*softly*). Yes.
> *She compares two red flowers, thoughtfully selects one and adds lightly.*

Bored to death.

GENERAL (*rising and stammering, like a bewildered boy*). But . . . I love you.

AGLAE. I'm sure you do. And I love you. That's why I made up my mind to tell you this. Because I still am in love with you. And because I vowed, the day I became your wife, always to be as transparent to you as a little piece of crystal.
> *She adds, still as softly.*

Men have often looked at me . . .

GENERAL. What?

AGLAE (*with a fleeting smile*). I'm pretty. Men always do have eyes for women. It's only other men who never notice it. There you are, talking politics or sport with your best friends. But your most devoted friend is only listening with half an ear, and from the corner of his eye he's watching me passing the teacups on the far side of the room.

GENERAL. And you never said a word about it? His name! Tell me his name this instant!

AGLAE (*still smiling*). Why bother you over so little? It's a woman's job to spare her man such trivial concerns. But the other evening, in the garden, when you were describing your 1940 campaign, I felt—(I don't know why, because I love that story and each time you tell it, I admire you for making yourself sound so sweetly ludicrous, instead of showing us how brave you really were)—but I felt lonely suddenly and chilly—as if I were quite wet with rain. I shivered. Someone was sitting on the bench beside me—he is a kind, sensitive person, I know, and perhaps he guessed my state of mind—he laid his hand gently over mine.

She smiles.

These things happen. And I would probably never have mentioned it had I not been aware, for the first time that evening, that I often felt the need to be soothed . . . and, as it were, to be made warm again.

A pause. The GENERAL *stands as if turned to stone. She goes on, in the same soft relentless voice.*

There. That's all. And it won't happen again, believe me. I won't look to any other man but you for understanding. I've given you back your little piece of glass. You can continue to look through it as before. The glass is crystal clear.

Darkness has fallen, gradually, as she was speaking. She goes on arranging her flowers with graceful, unhurried gestures, one last patch of light catching her white dress.

GENERAL (*in a murmur*). Yes, but it's razor sharp.

AGLAE (*turning to him with her clear eyes*). Isn't one honest little cut better than a hidden wound you leave to fester? Didn't you teach me that honor required that one should always speak the truth?

GENERAL (*hoarsely*). In theory, yes, beloved.

CURTAIN

ACT ONE

SCENE TWO

ACT ONE

SCENE TWO

The GENERAL'S *study, the same evening.* LEBELLUC, *the first arrival, is seated in an armchair. The* GENERAL *is pacing.*

GENERAL. Lebelluc, my sister—has lodged a complaint against you.

LEBELLUC. Your sister?

GENERAL (*shouting*). Don't attempt to deny the facts, sir! I know everything. And you ought to have realized by now that there are certain matters which I don't view lightly.

LEBELLUC. General, I think I can safely say that I have always behaved impeccably towards your sister.

GENERAL. Are you quite sure of that?

LEBELLUC (*after a slight hesitation*). Positive! Save for a second, by mistake.

GENERAL. No speeches. I want facts! First, the glint. She complained of a glint in your eye.

45]

LEBELLUC. A glint—what do you mean, a glint? Can I help it if my eyes sparkle?

> *The* GENERAL *looks at him impassively. He finally owns up.*

Well, it was the day we all made pancakes . . .

GENERAL. Pancakes are no excuse!

LEBELLUC. Your wife took us up to the linen room to fit us out with aprons. I was in fine spirits. We'd all had too much to drink. One always lunches far too well at your house.

GENERAL. Never mind the flattery!

LEBELLUC. I was first down in the kitchen. I see a rump bending over a stove. I take hold of its haunches—

GENERAL. Is that the way you carry on in my house? In other people's, yes, if you must—I'm no prude. But in mine!

LEBELLUC (*plaintively*). You asked me to be frank, General. I thought the rump belonged to the cook. She turns around —and oh, calamity—it was your sister. The cap and apron misled me. I take a step back. For more reasons than one, I think she's going to slap my face. She falls into my arms and whimpers "Christian." Well, what would you have done?

GENERAL. That's neither here nor there. She's my sister. I should probably have hit her.

LEBELLUC. You're a man of steel. But I'm the tender sort. I kissed her.

GENERAL (*bursts out laughing*). You fool! That's the last thing you should have done.

[46

LEBELLUC *starts to laugh as well. The* GENERAL *immediately stops and says severely.*

Don't make me laugh, Lebelluc, or I'll slap your face and we'll fight a duel over *that.*

LEBELLUC (*sheepishly*). It was stupid, I know. But I couldn't help myself. I've a weak character. Or perhaps I'm unstable.

GENERAL. No self-analysis in matters of honor! What then?

LEBELLUC. What do you mean—what then?

GENERAL. You admit you kissed her. Right. Then what?

LEBELLUC. But that's all!

GENERAL. Good. I want to believe you. I always trust human nature until I am proved wrong. I may say that's a policy that has brought a lot of disappointments.

> *He chuckles.*

Poor old Bise . . . I must say I suspected as much. My dear Lebelluc, however could you have walked into a trap like that, at your age?

LEBELLUC (*preening*). I do have a certain power over women . . . Yes, there's something about me that attracts them and makes them feel at ease at the same time—something . . . how shall I put it?—That soothes them, in a way. . . .

> *The* GENERAL *stiffens and looks at him suspiciously.*

GENERAL (*thoughtfully*). Soothes them, eh?

LEBELLUC. I admit it's weak of me. But if you had this power you'd do the same, General. It's a great temptation to use it. When I go to the cinema, for instance, in Paris, and I happen to be sitting next to an attractive girl (and pro-vided she is alone, of course; I don't believe in looking for trouble), I always reach for her hand, in the dark—just to see what happens. . . .

GENERAL (*moving closer and fingering his mustache*). Do you?

LEBELLUC (*oblivious of his danger*). In the first place, it makes the film go quicker. They're never very good these days. Have you noticed how the cinema is deteriorating? Now, the theatre, on the other hand—

GENERAL (*impatiently*). No cultural digressions! We were talking about women. Doesn't she take her hand away?

LEBELLUC. Who?

GENERAL. The girl in the cinema.

LEBELLUC. Not often, I must say. It's as if the touch of my hand in the dark gave her a sense of comfort. Women often need quietening a little, you know. They're so highly strung.

GENERAL. Yet you're pretty ugly, Lebelluc.

LEBELLUC. They don't seem to think so. You're a man, you obviously can't be aware of that little something I was telling you about. Now, as regards your sister—

GENERAL. Let's forget Bise now. That little matter is settled. Lebelluc, I'd like to ask you something. Do you recall my 1940 campaign?

LEBELLUC. Of course I do. You've told the story often enough. What about it?

GENERAL. The last time I so far forgot myself as to tell it, the other evening in the garden, were you with us, Lebelluc?

LEBELLUC. I was indeed. I remember it well. The evening was mild, the whisky mellow, the women delightful—

GENERAL. The women delightful, you say? Where exactly were you sitting?

LEBELLUC. Oh, I can't remember now.

GENERAL. Here is a rough layout of my garden furniture. I was here. Chair, trees, coffee table, chair, more trees, the bench, my wife. I want to know, you understand, to find out how my voice carries. You were sitting some way away from me, were you? On the bench—by my wife, perhaps?

LEBELLUC. I have the impression—

GENERAL. To hell with impressions! I want facts. Show me your seat!

> TARQUIN EDWARD MENDIGALES *comes bouncing in, wearing an apron and carrying a frying pan.*

MENDIGALES. General, your wife has just had an enchanting idea. We're all making pancakes. Won't you join us?

GENERAL. No thank you. I'll just eat them.

MENDIGALES. What about you, Monsieur Lebelluc? They tell me you're a great hand at pancakes.

GENERAL. He's a bit unstable for that sort of thing. He'll just eat them too.

MENDIGALES. What a shame! You'd enjoy it. Your wife can't stop laughing. You should see her, she's having a wonderful time. (*Exit*)

LEBELLUC (*a little sourly*). Enterprising boy, isn't he?

GENERAL. Very.

49]

LEBELLUC. I see he's keeping your wife amused.

GENERAL. Yes. He's moving in fast. Well, Lebelluc, was this your seat? You're taking your time over it.

LEBELLUC. Oh, I remember. I was sitting over there next to you. At one point, if you remember, you handed me your glass to indicate the rout of the High Command.

GENERAL. You've had a lucky escape, Lebelluc. It's a great thing to have a faithful memory.

Enter MICHEPAIN.

MICHEPAIN. Ta ra! Ta ra! Ta ra! The maggots are in the fruit! Squad 'shun! Michepain reporting for duty! Sir!

GENERAL (*a little irritated*). Good evening, Michepain.

MICHEPAIN. Ever since you did me the honor of approaching me about it, I've thought of nothing else, General. I've already drawn up a list applicable to the district.

GENERAL. A list of what?

MICHEPAIN. A list of maggots. And I don't move a step without my maggot detector. There's a lot more blows to be struck yet! Michepain, Sergeant, No. 1457839, reporting for duty! Sir!

GENERAL. All right, all right. At ease. You mustn't take everything literally, Michepain. We have to draw up a plan of campaign first.

MICHEPAIN. Right, General. Tactics are your province. You do the thinking. I'll stay quiet as a mouse till zero hour. I understand, sir! But at zero hour, not a second before, not a second later, Michepain is first over the top.

To LEBELLUC.

I love it when things start to hum, don't you?

[50

LEBELLUC (*tepidly*). Yes, yes . . .

MICHEPAIN. How many of us are there for this first meeting? If a mere Sergeant in the Reserve may make so bold as to ask, General?

GENERAL. Oh, it's hardly a mass movement yet. Anyway, I don't believe in mass movements. The future lies with active minorities.

MICHEPAIN. Active minorities!

GENERAL. Of course, we'll have to pad ours out a bit. I'm expecting Baron Belazor. The Doctor didn't seem too keen . . .

MICHEPAIN. Is he an anti-maggot man? I must say, General, he took very poor care of my sister last year, over her heartburn . . .

GENERAL. I don't see the connection. No, he didn't actually say no, but he says he has a lot of confinements at the moment. Still, I think I can talk him round.

MICHEPAIN. My daughter is very clever with her paintbrush. She could design us a banner.

GENERAL (*visibly irritated by* MICHEPAIN's *stupidity*). The banner can wait. We're still at the discussion stage.

MICHEPAIN (*dreamily*). The discussion stage . . .

GENERAL. We must be careful. If we call attention to ourselves too soon, we're finished.

MICHEPAIN. Finished. Yes, sir! No banner and a clamp on the tongue! After the victory of the movement, you can rely on me to go back into the ranks. Michepain never intrudes. I haven't a lot to say for myself. I love France, General, but I'm all piss and wind.

> *Stiffening to attention, apologetically.*

Between soldiers, General.

GENERAL. Quite, quite. At ease, at ease, man.

MICHEPAIN (*docilely*). At ease, sir.

> BELAZOR *comes hurrying in.*

BELAZOR. Good evening, Lulu!

GENERAL (*looking at his watch*). Henri, you are twenty-two minutes late.

BELAZOR (*not at all put out*). Only twenty-two minutes? Why, that's early for me. Good evening, Lebelluc.

LEBELLUC. Good evening, Belazor.

GENERAL (*introducing them*). Monsieur Michepain, our local ironmonger, who is one of our group. Baron Belazor.

MICHEPAIN. Good evening, Baron.

BELAZOR. Monsieur Michepain, the Baroness isn't too happy with her new saucepans. The enamel has chipped already. And she noticed, from their catalogue, that the hardware emporium in Paris sold them two hundred francs cheaper.

MICHEPAIN (*every inch an ironmonger*). It depends on the line of goods, sir. Now, your cheap enamel ware is bound to—

GENERAL. We haven't come here to discuss hardware, Henri.

BELAZOR. I'm sorry, Ludovic. Anyway, I don't give a damn for his pots and pans, nor for the Baroness either. Her enamel's chipping too. Yes, I know, she's an angel. But angels aren't good at growing old. Who is, I ask myself? I had a facial the other day, did I tell you? The results are sensational. Look at my lines.

    The GENERAL *looks, without comment.*

Oh, all right! You're as blind as a bat, anyway. I often wonder how you got into the Army. Anyway, the young woman who did the treatment is sheer heaven. A blonde, my dear—I cannot tell you! Strokes your face for twenty minutes for thirteen hundred francs. Can you wonder if one comes out ten years younger? How is that charming little wife of yours? How civilized of you, Lulu, to marry late in life and bring an adorable, brand-new little wife into the neighborhood. It was high time somebody did. There's a sad lack of pretty women hereabouts. Married ones I mean, of course. Pretty girls are ten a penny. But one has to pay one's court when Father isn't looking. Tell me, is she well?

GENERAL (*grunting*). Yes, yes, she's well. She's on top of the world at the moment.

BELAZOR. Is she? I'm so glad. I'm very fond of your wife. She was looking a little pent-up lately, I thought. Speaking as a friend, she's a little wisp of a thing who needs soothing, you know, Ludovic, once in a while. The least thing will do it, a kind word, a touch of the hand—

GENERAL (*thoughtfully*). Tell me, Henri . . . Excuse me, gentlemen, just a small private matter.

    Drawing him aside.

It sounds a silly question, but I'll explain later—Do you remember the other evening, in the garden, when I was telling the story of my 1940 campaign?

BELAZOR. I should say so!

GENERAL (*suspiciously*). Why should you say so?

BELAZOR. Why shouldn't I?

GENERAL. Stop hedging. I'm not asking you why you shouldn't have said, "I should say so," I want to know why you did say, "I should say so!"

BELAZOR. Don't you care for the expression?

GENERAL. Let's say it's your tone that offends me. You think I tell the story a bit too often too, do you? My wife said so to you, did she? I was a bit longwinded, eh? Be honest.

BELAZOR. Not a bit of it. It was wildly funny.

GENERAL (*Macchiavellian*). You amaze me. You kept shifting in your chair. A little uncomfortable, were you?

BELAZOR. Uncomfortable? Why should I be?

GENERAL. Some of my garden chairs are a bit rickety. Was your chair rickety?

BELAZOR. No . . .

GENERAL. Was it a bench or a chair? Try to be accurate.

BELAZOR. What the deuce do you want to know that for? I'm blessed if I can remember. I think it must have been a bench. Or a chair.

GENERAL. Well, which?

BELAZOR. Is it important?

GENERAL (*icily*). It might be.

> *Indicating the chairs.*
> *Enter the* DOCTOR.

DOCTOR. Do forgive me, gentlemen. I was attending the bailiff's wife over at the farm. It's a boy!

MICHEPAIN (*springing to attention*). *Vive la France!* One more little soldier!

GENERAL (*irritated*). At ease, Michepain.
>*To* BELAZOR, *treacherously.*
We'll discuss the matter later. Meanwhile perhaps you will have remembered exactly where you were sitting.
>*He gives him a stern look.*
I repeat—exactly. Let us join the others in the garden and discuss the basic policy of the movement.
>*He intercepts the* DOCTOR *and draws him aside.*
Oh, Doctor, there's something I wanted to ask you. Tell me, you did come here for coffee last week, didn't you?— Out in the garden?

DOCTOR. I did, General. Very good coffee it was too.

GENERAL. You're too kind. I couldn't quite place you. Where were you sitting, exactly?

DOCTOR. Let's see, near your wife, General, I think.

GENERAL. Ah. I'd like to have a little talk to you.
>*They go into the garden.*
>
>*After the* GENERAL *and the* DOCTOR *have gone, the cupboard door opens where* MARIE-CHRISTINE *has been eavesdropping. She signals* TOTO *and the* MILKMAN'S SON *to enter and join her. All three, armed with cap pistols and toy machine guns, sneak out following the conspirators. They go out.* TARQUIN EDWARD MENDIGALES, SOPHIE *and* AGLAE *come in, carrying on an animated conversation.*

MENDIGALES. Someone threw a bottle. The chandelier crashed

down into the oysters; the duchess found caviare inside her powder case. The manager called the police and we spent the night in jail, with prostitutes and petty crooks!

SOPHIE. Oh, Paris must be such fun!

AGLAE. I've been there many times, but nothing so amusing ever happened to me.

MENDIGALES. If you stay at a stuffy family hotel and spend your evenings at the Comédie Française you can't complain if Paris seemed the tiniest bit provincial. Next time you make the trip, let me know, I'll come too. You'll meet the most entrancing company Paris has to offer. Abstract painters, perverts, communists, ballet dancers, a world-famous poet thief, a fantastic Dominican monk who smokes opium. Who else?—Two or three crown princes, a wildly handsome cycling champion who's the friend of a famous dress designer—no names! And all very progressive of course, the whole thing. We stay up half the night discussing the future of the world. You'll have a fabulous time. You must live, girls!

SOPHIE (*clinging to his arm*). Will you teach us, Tarquin Edward?

MENDIGALES. Of course! That's why Fate brought me to this forgotten hole. I came to be your rescuer! We are going to stir this place into a froth!

AGLAE. I don't think you'll find it very easy.

MENDIGALES. Leave it to me. I have a plan.
He produces a script.

SOPHIE. What's that?

MENDIGALES. Wait and see.

AGLAE. What is it?

MENDIGALES. A play. I saw it last season in Paris. If this doesn't make them sit up, nothing will.

AGLAE. Do you mean you want us to act in it?

SOPHIE. But we couldn't! Father would never let us.

MENDIGALES. Nonsense. All we need is an excuse. I know! We'll do it for Charity! There must be an annual Charity Fete in this backwater.

AGLAE. The 2nd of August, on St. Alphonso's Day.

MENDIGALES. Perfect. Is there a hall we can use?

AGLAE. We could do it in the garden.

SOPHIE. But who would we have in it? We don't know anyone around here under ninety.

MENDIGALES. Do you know Pinsac? He's a neighbor of yours.

AGLAE. My husband doesn't speak to him for political reasons.

MENDIGALES. What about Achille de Lepaud?

AGLAE. He says Achille de Lepaud is a dreadful little playboy.

MENDIGALES. Of course he is! That's why he's such fun! You'll adore him.

SOPHIE. Tarquin Edward, if you can persuade Father to let us put on a play you must be very, very clever.

MENDIGALES. Leave the General to me, I'll handle him. I'm a past-master at strategy too, you know.
       He takes their arms and starts to lead them off.
Come along. Let's go in the garden.

AGLAE. But what about your factory? How will you find time to rehearse and organize it all? You said your father—

57]

MENDIGALES. Isn't she a love! I've mastered the art of taming fathers, you can be sure of that! They're our "old husbands" in a way!

SOPHIE (*shrieking with laughter as she goes out*). Tarquin Edward! Aglae won't like you if you talk like that! She adores my father!

MENDIGALES. I adore mine! That needn't stop us having fun, need it?

> *They go out.* MARIE-CHRISTINE *comes charging in, clutching a toy machine gun, followed by* TOTO *with a little wooden sword. With a great show of stealth she drags* TOTO *over to the conservatory doors, then with a sudden whoop pulls back the curtain and peppers the conspirators with the machine gun. At the same time, the* MILKMAN'S BOY *charges in through the garden windows with the rat-tat-tat of machine guns and cries of "Down with the Germans!" The conspirators take refuge inside the room. There follows a short skirmish, during which the* GENERAL, *aided by* BELAZOR, *rounds on the children, pulls them off* LEBELLUC *and* MICHEPAIN *and kicks them out of the room.*

GENERAL. Let's come back inside. With those children running about we can't possibly discuss anything. This absurd mania children have for playing at war! Now, gentlemen, we're all agreed, I think. Our first task is to restore to France the taste for austerity, discipline and hard work!

DOCTOR. We're all agreed on that, General. But how?

GENERAL. How? Let us proceed point by point. First, let's agree on basic principles. That will be something.

[58

BELAZOR. The only thing is, dear fellow, everybody has principles. And for some extraordinary reason, which no one has yet been able to explain, they're always more or less identical. Everybody wants peace and universal happiness —yet everybody goes to war. So I ask you, where are you? If you can understand that you're a genius.

GENERAL. To hell with understanding! People have been trying to understand for far too long! If the world is to be saved at all, it will be saved by fools.

MICHEPAIN. At your service, sir!

GENERAL. At ease, Michepain!

MICHEPAIN. I would just like to say one thing if I may.

GENERAL. What is it?

MICHEPAIN. It's about the maggots.

GENERAL. Ah—

MICHEPAIN. I've given them a lot of thought lately. You'll never believe it, General, but even in hardware, you get maggots. In the old days, hardware was cut and dried, it was honest, it was clean. A saucepan was a saucepan. But the maggots have crept into it. Color, fancy knobs, plastic trimmings—a woman chooses her stewing pot the way she chooses a hat! I'm in hardware, I shouldn't be saying this, but the secret of a good sauce, as everybody knows, is a wooden spoon. But these days? Rubbish, that's what they're selling! Push-button gadgets that do the work while Madam watches television. And if they fall to pieces a year later, all the better. You buy another. It makes for a quick turnover, which is all your maggot cares about. You'll say I ought to be pleased about it; I'm not in business for my

health. Pardon me, I am not pleased. Turnover isn't everything. There's honor. Hardware is hardware. It's not fancy
goods. A saucepan is a saucepan. It's sacred. There. I've
said my say. From now on, I'll keep my mouth shut and
wait for zero hour.

GENERAL. Thank you, Michepain. I have allowed Michepain
to speak at length, gentlemen, because he represents the
spirit of the old-time craftsmen. To begin with, the world
is in chaos because man has lost his roots. What I want to
do is to wean man back to his home and family, and restore
his allegiance to his trade.

DOCTOR. Oh, come, come! You're 200 years out of date.
Modern man has broken loose and he wants more out of
life than home and family. I can tell you that now! And
what about free love? And women's emancipation? And
the third sex— What are you going to do with that?

GENERAL. Nothing at all! We had enough trouble with the
other two.

BELAZOR. Oh, come off it. You aren't going to pass a law
forcing us to sleep exclusively with our wives, dammit!

GENERAL. I might at that.

BELAZOR. Look, little Lulu, I have a feeling we're going off the
rails a bit.

GENERAL (*exploding*). To begin with, I am not your little
Lulu! We may have wet our pants together when we were
four years old, but that doesn't make me your little Lulu!

BELAZOR. All right, all right. Motion carried. You're not my
Lulu. In future, if you want, I'll give you your proper rank.

GENERAL. I should hope so! Everything's far too free and easy! I want life to become difficult again; I want us to pay for everything, out of our own pockets, to pay for love, to pay for liberty and pay dearly; not to have them for the asking by simply filling in a form! And I want us to go back to calling one another "sir"!

DOCTOR. Now, I really must interrupt here. Will you deny that the happiness of the greatest number has become one of our fundamental social concepts?

GENERAL. I don't know what the greatest number means. I know men, as individuals, that's all. There are good ones and there are mediocre ones. That's the yardstick of my interest in them. Tell me, Doctor, is a fool sacred to you?

DOCTOR. No. . . . Why?

GENERAL. Two fools are one fool plus another fool. They're still not sacred. And a thousand fools are 999 fools plus another for good measure. I fail to see by what mathematical law this agglomeration of fools should become increasingly sacred the larger it becomes.

DOCTOR. But that's blasphemy! The masses—

GENERAL. Who are they?

DOCTOR. What do you mean—who are they?

GENERAL. Never met them. Have you? Who introduced you? Where?

DOCTOR. A joke isn't an answer.

LEBELLUC. General, I don't think we are quite with you. Let's have some light on the subject.

61]

BELAZOR. That's it, little Lulu. Light your lantern and don't get excited.

GENERAL. Your little Lulu will get excited if he feels like it, sir! You're all looking at me with shocked disapproval because I don't appear to believe in the sanctity of the greatest number. So I'm going to ask you to explain a myth which, I must say, has always puzzled me. Let me take a concrete example. A workman falls off a roof and breaks his neck. One corpse: two lines in the evening paper. Nobody bothers to read it. A trawler sinks off the coast of Brittany. Twelve dead. We don't sidle up to each other and say, "Did you read about such and such in the paper today," but we give it a passing thought. A train crashes. 120 dead. Ah, now we're getting somewhere! Now we start to look sad. "Did you read about that train smash?" "Dreadful, dreadful." Now *why* do we look so sad? Why has it suddenly become dreadful?

LEBELLUC. Because there are 120 dead!

GENERAL. Really? And do 120 dead make you, personally, feel sad, Lebelluc?

LEBELLUC. Obviously.

GENERAL. Much sadder than twelve dead? You didn't look so sad over the trawler.

LEBELLUC. Well no, it stands to reason . . .

GENERAL. Why? Why does it stand to reason? Do you have a pair of scales inside you to weigh the dead with, Lebelluc? How sensitive is it? One dead man doesn't register. Twelve dead, it starts to move. A hundred and twenty dead—presto, the scales tip!—You're sad. But then, eighty dead must have made you a tiny bit less sad, mustn't it, if your scales are working properly?

DOCTOR. General, this isn't argument, it's verbal gymnastics!

GENERAL. Explain yourself.

DOCTOR. The death of one unknown man doesn't mean very much to us, true enough. But a hundred dead disturbs us profoundly, because our sense of human brotherhood comes into play—

GENERAL. And the poor, solitary workman who fell off his roof, all by himself? Wasn't he your brother? If he'd had the wit to drag his 999 workmates off the scaffolding with him, would that give him the right to call himself your brother? What kind of morality is that?

BELAZOR. Listen, Lulu, you're just playing with words now. A hundred dead isn't just a number, don't forget. It's a hundred families, Lord knows how many orphans, a hundred weeping widows—

GENERAL. I see, so a lot of tears affects you more than a few tears? How many gallons of tears does it take before you feel sad?

BELAZOR. Don't be such a bore with your tears! It's absurd. I'm talking about the grief of widows and orphans, old darling.

GENERAL. Very well, sir. Your old darling will now consider the widows. So, Belazor, my tender heart, two widows are sadder than one widow, is that it?

BELAZOR. A bit sadder, yes.

GENERAL. Why?

63]

BELAZOR. Well . . . because there are two of them.

GENERAL. So four widows are twice as sad as two widows, if I've got you right?

BELAZOR (*less sure*). Yes . . .

GENERAL. And if I ask you why, you'll say: because there are four of them?

BELAZOR. Yes. No. Perhaps. Oh, I don't know!

GENERAL. Let's move on to large figures, so we'll see how your sensibility reacts. 7,392 widows for instance, to take a small incident in the last war—that seems sadder to you, if I've followed you, than 6,867 widows. And you heave a sigh of relief when you learn that the High Command had made a mistake in their original estimate. 425 widows less, that's quite a treat. Even in wartime.

BELAZOR (*uneasily*). I don't know. Yes. I suppose so.

GENERAL. Now, 1,900,625 widows—

BELAZOR (*exploding*). Oh, to hell with your widows! What are you trying to do—prove that I'm a fool?

GENERAL (*quietly*). No, Belazor, my old friend. A man. A man who has no weighing machine in his heart with which to count sorrowing widows. A real man to whom numbers mean nothing. Because, in fact, numbers do mean nothing. Only nobody has the guts to say so.

> *For some time now,* MICHEPAIN *has been lifting a finger in an attempt to get a word in. The* GENERAL *sees him.*

GENERAL. What is it, Michepain? Do you want to pee?

MICHEPAIN. I was only going to say that to my mind there's

[64

something even sadder than a hundred widows; and that's one widower. I mean to say, women can always get along in life, whereas a man on his own, if only for the food . . .

The others roar with laughter at this.

GENERAL. Gentlemen—please. The time for amusement is over.

> AGLAE *appears in the doorway, surrounded by* MENDIGALES, SOPHIE *and* BISE. *The* GENERAL *goes to her, his anger gone.*

AGLAE. My dear, I've come to act as spokesman for a little conspiracy.

> *The* GENERAL *and his friends give a start.*

GENERAL. Conspiracy? What conspiracy?

AGLAE (*smiling*). Only about the annual Charity Fete. It was Monsieur Mendigales' idea. We've decided to put on a play for St. Alphonso's Day.

GENERAL. Now just a minute—!

AGLAE (*with a winning smile*). I thought we might put it on in the garden.

SOPHIE (*clapping her hands*). Oh, yes, Papa! Thank you, Papa!

GENERAL. Yes, Papa! Thank you, Papa! Not so fast— I haven't said yes!

BISE. Monsieur Mendigales assures us that he'll persuade you to act in it yourself!

GENERAL. Me? With flour on my face and a false beard! Not on your life!

BISE. It's for Charity, Ludovic!

MENDIGALES. You're our bright hope, sir! The entire neighborhood will flock to see you.

GENERAL. That's the last thing I want.

MENDIGALES. And these gentlemen must be in it too.

DOCTOR. Splendid! I was quite a hand at theatricals at school.

BELAZOR. So was I! Do you remember Lulu, when we— } *Together*

LEBELLUC. What a good idea! We could do with a little entertainment, eh, General?

GENERAL. I can think of nothing more repellent.

MENDIGALES. I'm convinced you'll change your mind, sir. Allow me to give you a taste of it.

AGLAE. Yes, why doesn't Monsieur Mendigales read it to us?

SOPHIE. Oh, yes!

BELAZOR. Come on, Lulu, don't be such a killjoy. } *Together*

AGLAE. Let's all sit down, shall we?
                Holding out her hand.
Ludovic, my dear—

GENERAL (*defeated*). Very well, since my wife seems set on the idea. Oh, Doctor, come and sit next to my wife, like you were the other evening in the garden.

DOCTOR. I wasn't sitting next to your wife, General. I remember now, I was sitting next to your sister.

LEBELLUC. And very nice too!

[66

BELAZOR (*to the* GENERAL). I wonder what the theatre is up to nowadays.

GENERAL. I've no idea. I never go near the place.

AGLAE. That's nothing to boast about, my dear.

MENDIGALES. I agree, General. You really should keep in touch. The modern drama has taken a great stride forward. Entertainment for its own sake is a thing of the past.

GENERAL. Is it? Why? Mustn't we have fun any more?

MENDIGALES. Living as we are under the threat of atomic destruction, we temporary inhabitants of this planet have no time for that. The task before us is to deepen the awareness of man, by man, for man—and in human terms. Which does not, as you will see, in any way preclude metaphysical anguish, nor a kind of desperate humor.

GENERAL. It sounds like a cheerful evening. But you know we've always been more or less temporary inhabitants of this planet. That didn't stop us having a good laugh now and then.

AGLAE (*sitting on the arm of his chair and taking his hand*). Ludovic dear, I'm so longing to hear this play. You don't want to spoil that pleasure for me, do you?

GENERAL. Not for anything in the world, my love. Right, young man, begin.

MENDIGALES. The play is entitled *Bing-Bong*.

GENERAL. Bing Bong.

MENDIGALES. An anti-drama.

GENERAL. Anti-drama.

LEBELLUC. Why?

MENDIGALES. You'll see in a second. It's a Popopief play.

BELAZOR. Who's he?

MENDIGALES. One of the shining lights of the Paris scene.

SOPHIE. Popopief . . .

LEBELLUC. You know— Popopief!

MENDIGALES. I'll read you the opening scene so you can get the feel of it.

SOPHIE. Paris, Paris, Paris at last!

MENDIGALES. *Bing-Bong.*

GENERAL. Anti-drama.

MENDIGALES. The set represents nothing.

GENERAL. Good.

MENDIGALES. "Left, a door boarded up with rough planks. U.S.C.: a window set too high to see out of. Center stage: a bidet."

BISE (*not sure if she has heard right*). A what?

LEBELLUC. You know—
He illustrates.

MENDIGALES (*firmly*). This object, as you will see, has a profound metaphysical significance.
Reading.
"Julian and Apophasia are crouching side by side on the floor. They do not speak. They do not move. There is complete, utter and engulfing silence."
A pause. His listeners wait expectantly. MENDI-

GALES *stands with his script in his hand, looking into space. The* GENERAL *stares at him blankly.*

GENERAL. So?

MENDIGALES. That's it.

GENERAL. What's it?

MENDIGALES. That is the kernel of the whole play. The rest is in fact an elaboration of that basic point. "The two characters crouch there, looking vacant. The pause must continue until the audience can bear it no longer."

GENERAL. I think we've reached that point.

MENDIGALES. General, I don't think you understand. It's a moment of quite shattering audacity. It's the first time in the history of drama that the curtain goes up and absolutely nothing happens! There's something about it that catches at your throat! It shows one the utter nothingness of man, his uselessness, the gaping void within him. It's quite hair-raisingly significant.

GENERAL. Go on.

MENDIGALES. "Julian: You whore!"

BISE (*shocked*). Ooh!

MENDIGALES. We could change that to prostitute if you like. But it's terribly important. It's the key to the whole drama of the man-woman relationship.

LEBELLUC (*to* MENDIGALES). Do go on.

MENDIGALES. "Julian: Prostitute. Put out the light. Apophasia: There's never been a light. Julian: Leave it on then." An anguished pause. "Julian: Nothing. There is nothing. Nothing has ever happened anywhere and nothing ever will. So what's the use of going on?"

GENERAL. Balderdash! I think we've heard enough, young man! I prefer to believe that you're thumbing your nose at us. That's the least painful supposition. And you seriously imagined that I would slap paint on my face to act such asinine gibberish as that? Why, it's unadulterated pig swill.

MENDIGALES. General, that is the drama of tomorrow.

GENERAL. Then save it for tomorrow! I'm not having it here! Get out of my house! And take that piece of driveling infantilism with you! Get out!
> *To conspirators.*

All of you! Go and play your demented parlor games somewhere else! If you want to behave like a lot of feebleminded children, go and do it outside and leave me in peace. I've got work to do!
> *They all go out save* AGLAE.

AGLAE. Ludovic—please.

GENERAL. Never! Never! Well, we'll see. But not *that* play!

AGLAE. Thank you!
> *She exits. The* GENERAL *takes an enormous piece of Ministafia from the desk and gobbles it.*

CURTAIN

ACT TWO

ACT TWO

The grounds. In the background, under the trees, the open-air theatre is in the process of being fitted up. A red curtain, partly fixed in position, hangs in front of the little stage. Wicker settees and armchairs around a statue on the lawn. On a chair, a portable gramophone is playing a popular waltz. Alone onstage, AGLAE, *looking like one of Goya's Spanish ladies, in the white dress she will wear for the play, is waltzing with eyes closed, to the music.*

Enter TOTO. *He looks at her for a second or two in silence.*

TOTO. Mamma?

AGLAE (*still dancing with her eyes closed*). Yes?

TOTO. Shall I wear my yellow jersey?

AGLAE (*still dancing*). Yes, darling.

TOTO. If we're having guests, shouldn't I wear the white one?

AGLAE. Yes, darling.

TOTO. There's a hole in it, though.

AGLAE. Yes, darling.

TOTO. Shall I ask Julia to mend it?

ALGAE. Yes, darling.

>   *She is still waltzing.* TOTO *hesitates, then asks.*

TOTO. Mamma?

AGLAE. Yes, darling?

TOTO. Mlle. Tromph will be here soon and she said I had to learn my seven times table by heart.

AGLAE (*still waltzing*). That's right, darling, you must.

TOTO (*a bit crestfallen*). Can I recite it to you?

AGLAE. What, darling?

TOTO. My seven times table.

AGLAE (*dancing*). Of course, darling.

TOTO.
>   7 x 1 is 7.
>   7 x 2 is 14.
>   7 x 3 is . . .
>   *He stops.*

AGLAE.
>   21.

TOTO.
>   7 3's is 21.
>   7 4's is 28.
>   7 5's is 34.

[74

AGLAE.

7 5's is 35.

TOTO.

7 5's is 35.
7 6's is 36.
7 7's is 37.
7 8's is 38.
7 9's is 39.
7 10's is 40.
Mamma, did I do it right?

AGLAE (*waltzing*). Yes, darling, quite right.
> *The* GENERAL *has come in a moment or so before, looking slightly grotesque in his theatre costume. He has been listening, amazed, to this curious arithmetic lesson.*

TOTO. See you later, Mamma. I'm going out to play now.
> *He skips out without seeing the* GENERAL.

AGLAE. Enjoy yourself, darling.
> *She is still dancing. The record stops. She waltzes around a few more times with her eyes closed, then stops. She opens her eyes and sees the* GENERAL *directly in front of her.*

Oh! You startled me.

GENERAL. You were dancing?

AGLAE. I was hearing Toto's multiplication tables.

GENERAL. While you were dancing?

AGLAE. Yes, while I was dancing. I love that waltz. Monsieur Mendigales gave me the record. He says it's all the rage in Paris this season.

75]

GENERAL. Paris is behind the times. That waltz came out in my day. I learned to dance to it as a cadet, with the battalion sergeant. All they've done is add a trumpet to it. I can't imagine why.

AGLAE (*smiling*). You are incorrigible.

> AGLAE *has put the record on again. She goes on dancing, by herself.*

Will our play be a success, do you think?

GENERAL. Now we've gone this far it had better be, or we'll all look pretty silly.

AGLAE (*dancing*). You know, Ludovic, I'm very glad we're doing this one instead. I didn't like to say so, but I didn't care for that first play very much. This one is infinitely more poetic. *The Loves of Donna Ardela and Rosario—* Isn't that a lovely title? Monsieur Mendigales says it was adapted from old Andalusian by a young Spaniard who earns his living as a doorman in a nightclub in Montmartre.

GENERAL. Very touching, I'm sure. But it adds nothing to the piece—which is charming, by the way. A bit pretentious in spots, but it's growing on me. Aglae, stop dancing.

> *He turns off the gramophone.*

AGLAE (*opening her eyes*). Why?

GENERAL. I don't like you dancing by yourself with your eyes closed. I wonder who you are with.

AGLAE (*smiling*). Would you rather I danced with my eyes open, in some young man's arms?

GENERAL. Yes! No. I don't know.

AGLAE (*gently, still smiling*). That's a pleasure that's forbidden me, you know that.

[76

GENERAL. Not by me at all events. Now that we've started the round of pleasure, there's no reason why we should stop. I'm giving a ball in the autumn on the feast of Saint . . . Oh well, we'll find some saint or other.

AGLAE (*laughing an odd little laugh*). There's a treat in store! And we'll ask Lebelluc, I suppose, and Friselaine, and the Doctor?

> *She goes on more seriously.*

No, you don't forbid it, I know. You're a very intelligent, generous husband. But I do.

GENERAL. Why?

AGLAE. Because I'm your wife and I mean to be faithful in my most secret thoughts, just as I swore to be.

> *She moves into his arms.*

Why don't you ever dance with me? Put the record on again and let's dance.

GENERAL. In the arms of my sergeant instructor, I had a certain grace, they tell me. But today, in yours, I should look like a great grisly bear.

AGLAE. Let's try.

> *She starts the gramophone and takes him in her arms. The* GENERAL *dances a few halting steps with her and then stops.*

GENERAL. No, Aglae. I want to talk to you.

AGLAE (*very slightly irked*). What about? I have a feeling that you want to reopen the conversation we had the other day. The subject is closed and I assure you it won't have a sequel.

GENERAL. No. We won't mention that again.

77]

AGLAE (*sitting down obediently*). Very well. Begin. There, you see? I'm sitting down like a schoolgirl ready for her lessons.

GENERAL. Don't make fun of me. What I have to say isn't easy.

AGLAE. Make fun of you? You know far more than I do about everything.

GENERAL (*softly*). I'm not so sure I do, now.

AGLAE (*mischievously*). Proceed with the orders, General. I'm listening. Only don't make me stand to attention. I'm a little tired.

GENERAL. Don't laugh at me. Giving orders is easy in a system that holds water. The Army handbooks are very cut and dried. But the civilian handbooks seem to me infinitely less specific. And I wouldn't, for anything in the world, lose this war. My last.

AGLAE. What war?

GENERAL. Our war, Aglae.

AGLAE (*gently, in genuine surprise*). Whatever gave you the idea we were at war?

GENERAL. A man and a woman who have attempted to share life and to love each other—two things that are often contradictory—are nearly always at war, Aglae, secretly.

    A *pause*.

AGLAE. You are my husband. I vowed I would be a good wife to you and I will be, always. There is no war and no problem. This is peace. The sweet peace of uneventfulness and growing children and successful harvests.

GENERAL. And of good little schoolgirls sitting demurely in their chairs, while the look in their eyes grows more and more remote. You mustn't think me stupider than I am, Aglae.

AGLAE (*quickly*). I should never have told you I was bored, the other evening. I wish I hadn't.

GENERAL. I know there's a touch of the grotesque about me. My fits of rage and my strictness irritate you a little, I know. I *am* strict and that's a virtue, but I tend to make other people pay for it a little. You see? I'm quite self-aware, aren't I? Why do you smile?

AGLAE. I love your tirades, and your indignant rages too, Ludovic, even when I don't altogether share them. You know what a weak, shallow man my father was. It was partly your scolding self-discipline I loved you for. When I was twelve, you know, I was passionately in love with a Spartan Hero, in a history book.

GENERAL. Girls always fall in love with a Hero, to begin with. "At last," they say to themselves, "here's a man who isn't like the rest of them." And they always betray him in the end, with a man who is exactly like the rest. It's a law of life.

AGLAE. That's in bad taste, my dear. I shall never be untrue to you.

GENERAL. Because you love me too much to do so, Aglae? Or because you love truth too much? There is a kind of fidelity which is only to oneself.

> *A pause. Then* AGLAE *says, quietly, unpenetrably.*

79]

AGLAE. I love truth.

A *pause*.

GENERAL (*in a hoarse murmur*). Why have you changed, Aglae?

AGLAE (*with a light, mysterious little laugh*). What a question! I don't know. Why do flowers always grow the same number of petals they were meant to have? Why does the wind blow on their pollen suddenly one day? Why? Why? Why? Those are questions children ask. Mother, why does everything grow and change and die? To children you answer, "Because."

GENERAL (*with a sudden cry*). I don't want anything to change, ever!

AGLAE (*with a clear, unmalicious little laugh*). How funny you are. You made up your mind, years ago, just how things ought to be—not only me, but France, human nature, everything! Beautiful, pure, strong, eternal, like in your schoolboy books. And if something decays or sprouts into bud, if something stirs or lives, if there's the least disarray in your lovely tidy edifice, you fly into a terrible rage. The rage of a disappointed little boy. And you run into your mother's arms. But there! Mamma has changed too. Like everything else that lives and breathes on earth. You must come back to earth, Ludovic, and make the best of it. You'll plot and plan less, nobody will want to put you into prison, you'll be more lovable and in the long run less unhappy.

GENERAL. I don't want to be lovable.

AGLAE (*smiling*). I know. Yet you want to be loved. You see how illogical you are.

GENERAL. I don't want to be loved!

AGLAE (*with a little laugh which has a slight edge to it this time*). Then what are you complaining about?

GENERAL (*suddenly hoarse*). I'm complaining about the fact that you don't love me any more.

AGLAE. I thought you didn't want to be loved?

GENERAL (*dully*). Not by others. By you, I do.

AGLAE. Anyway, that isn't true. I do love you, I told you so.

GENERAL. Not enough.

AGLAE (*smiling*). As best I can. You say I've changed. It's possible. You took me as a very young girl. You made a woman of me. That's a little phenomenon that men will never learn to accept. You're always battling against the inevitable. Forever tilting at windmills. The windmills go on turning. France and I continue to change.

GENERAL (*humbly*). Tell me the truth, Aglae.

AGLAE. You know how dangerous it is to ask me that. With other women it's safe enough. They alter the truth to suit the moment. With me it's terribly unwise. I simply tell it.

GENERAL. If one day you were attracted by another man, would you be unfaithful to me?

AGLAE (*distinctly*). No.

GENERAL. Why not?

AGLAE. Because I vowed I never would be.

GENERAL (*witheringly*). Because you vowed you never would be! Do you take me for an idiot, my little girl? Do you think any man could sleep peacefully under that leaky roof?

81]

You made a vow? Be damned to your vows! I want you to stay faithful to me because you love me! And if some young puppy takes your fancy, I'll say more! I hope and trust that you will be unfaithful to me!

AGLAE (*shrugging*). You don't know what you're saying.

GENERAL. I know perfectly well what I'm saying. And I'll go further! If somebody takes your hand, in the dark, out in the garden—

AGLAE (*gently, but firmly*). Ludovic.

GENERAL. —I'm not asking you who— I'll find out soon enough! But if some young fool excites you—or soothes you, as you put it— I'll thank you to go all the way! Otherwise it would be too easy! The romantic heroine in a cheap novel with her precious virtue still intact! Well, I won't have it! Damn you, take your courage in both hands and be unfaithful! It will be less humiliating. Up to me to fight back. Up to me to teach the pair of you that you want to be careful of men in roaring middle age! To begin with, I'm not acting in the play!

> AGLAE *moves away, quite calm, and puts the record on again.*

AGLAE. You're stabbing yourself with your own knife, Ludovic.

GENERAL. Up to the hilt! And let the blood spurt. That's my way.

AGLAE (*starting to dance*). Shall I disarm you with a word?

GENERAL (*with a snort*). A word? I doubt if you could. It takes more than a word to disarm me.

AGLAE (*still dancing*). I shall not be unfaithful to you, because I promised not to be. I shudder at the very thought of you as a wronged husband.

> *She stops dancing for a second. She is standing behind him. She says, distinctly.*

But if one day I fall in love with someone else, I shall tell you before he touches me, and I'll go away with him next day. There. I didn't swear to that, but I am sure.

GENERAL (*suddenly transfixed*). Aglae. My little bird . . .

> *A pause.*

AGLAE (*gently*). I told you you should never ask the truth of me. You must see to it that I don't fall in love with someone else, that's all.

> *She starts to dance again, her thoughts elsewhere.*

GENERAL (*rising*). I'll be amusing. I'll make you laugh. I'll give parties. I'll learn to dance again. I'll act in the play and in the last scene I'll go down on all fours and let you beat me with a stick, the way Monsieur Mendigales has it in the script.

> *He does a grotesque little dance and falls to his knees in front of her. She looks at him, amused, and says composedly.*

AGLAE. I don't like it when you force me to be a woman. We have a rarer relationship, you and I. Don't rob me of the pleasure of respecting you.

> *Changing her tone.*

We rehearse in half an hour. You've quite upset me. I shan't be able to act my part. And that comedy at least must be well played. I'll be back.

> *She goes swiftly out. The GENERAL gazes after her, helplessly. Enter LEBELLUC.*

83]

LEBELLUC. Good afternoon, General. I'm early. I'm worried to death about my role. I don't feel I've brought the character out, quite.

GENERAL (*suddenly*). Lebelluc! Have you known many women?

LEBELLUC (*guardedly*). Yes . . . no! What are you driving at now? Ever since the other evening, you've had me worried.

GENERAL (*humbly*). I know so little about them. When you feel something change for the first time—a tone of voice, a look . . .

LEBELLUC. My dear man, you smoke cigars, don't you? At the first bitter puff, throw it away. If you persist, through laziness or meanness, you'll just upset your stomach. After all, there are plenty more in the box to give you a fresh pleasure. Same with women.

GENERAL (*discouraged*). I don't think we're talking about quite the same thing, Lebelluc.

Enter BELAZOR.

BELAZOR. Listen, Lulu, you know my second-act scene with the Captain? I do believe I've got it. It's a great thing, acting! It comes so much more naturally than real life. Ah, there you are, Lebelluc. Shall we do our scene? Let's walk it, over on the lawn. I want to put the gestures in. "How sir!"

LEBELLUC. Now, sir!

BELAZOR. Fie, sir!

LEBELLUC. Why, sir! Do you know that I could slice your ears off with my sword, sir?

BELAZOR. Do you know that I could slice yours too, sir?

LEBELLUC. Let us try reason, sir!

BELAZOR. Yes, sir!

LEBELLUC. No, sir!

BELAZOR. Yes, sir!

> *They go out, gesticulating. The* GENERAL *is left alone.*

GENERAL. Yes, sir! No, sir! Yes, sir! No, sir! I'll cut your ears off, by God I will! And something else besides, to make some cuff links with! No, it's too stupid. A name, that's all I need to know! Great God, it's simple enough! Who in Satan's name was here that evening? The bench.

> *He puts it in place.*

My wife. Bise. Doctor. Friselain. Lebelluc. That ass Belazor. The pair of them were exchanging smutty stories all the time I was talking, he's already admitted that. I can just see him, leaning back, preening himself, pretending to listen to my story. Then he leans forward.

> *He does so.*

Who the flaming hell was sitting there? What a fool! It was me! Wrong track. Start again. Doctor. Friselain. Lebelluc. Belazor. Old Bise.

> *The* PRIEST *comes in and looks at him curiously as he tries all the chairs in turn, muttering as he does so.*

PRIEST. What are you doing, General? Are you working out a plan of campaign?

GENERAL. I'm trying to find out who was sitting on this bench last Wednesday evening after dinner.

PRIEST (*mildly*). Why, I was!

> *The* GENERAL *stands there speechless and stares at him. A pause. The* PRIEST *is still smiling.*

GENERAL (*in a strangled voice*). I know this is the day for revelations, but even so— You aren't going to tell me it was you who held my wife's hand in the dark, Father?

PRIEST. Yes, it was. But how did you manage to see me? I'd taken great care nobody should.

GENERAL. She told me. She didn't say who.

PRIEST. Forgive me, my friend, but I felt so sorry for her that evening. She had carefully carried out her little duties as a hostess, handed round the coffee cups and asked each guest "how many lumps," and then she'd taken her place, a little prisoner, amongst us all. You were talking away and out of the darkness came bursts of music and the sound of laughter as Sophie and her young friends danced on the lawn. I couldn't see her eyes as they gazed into the distance, but I could sense the look in them. And I suddenly realized that it was over there, among the silly laughter and the excitement of the darkness, that she should have been —not here with us. At one point she shivered slightly, for no reason—for it was a mild evening. And I laid my hand on hers so she should know that one person at least had guessed her secret.

> *A pause. Then the* GENERAL *asks in a cracked voice.*

GENERAL. Do you think she's unhappy?

PRIEST. I think she has, as they say—everything to bring her happiness. But I think—particularly in the case of women —that that doesn't always suffice to make them happy.

GENERAL. Do you think I ought to entertain her more?

PRIEST. Perhaps. Women have a special need to be amused. But you know, although they seem to demand the earth, deep down they don't ask for very much. A little life around them, a little warmth, a little pleasure.

GENERAL. Yes, Tarquin Edward Mendigales and his fatuous playboy jokes, that's what they want! His imbecilic friends and their shrieks of laughter over nothing. The froth of life! They live on froth!

PRIEST (*gently*). Don't speak ill of pleasure. God gave it to us along with the rest.

GENERAL. Yes. For dessert. Not for the main course.
 With a sudden cry.
But I love her, Father! I'd tear my insides out for her!

PRIEST (*kindly*). Why not give her a few sweetmeats instead?
 A pause.

GENERAL. How does one set about it? Do you know? I don't think I have ever known.

PRIEST. Imagine you're an explorer, who's brought back a little baby panther from the tropics. Play with her as you would a kitten, bring her tidbits of raw meat and lumps of sugar every day; keep her sometimes on a leash and let her frolic sometimes. Tickle her ears and let her lick you with her rough little tongue. But never forget that one fine day, adore you though she does, she may smell blood, wake up a full-grown panther and strike you dead with one stroke of her paw.
 He stops, a little flustered, and adds primly.

I am not, of course, referring to the noble ideal of the Christian wife and mother.

GENERAL (*clapping him on the shoulder*). Ah, Father . . . And to think that old rake Lebelluc could only talk to me about cigars! How did you come to know so much about women?

PRIEST. Oh, it's all theoretical, you know . . .

GENERAL. They're coming to rehearse. Shall I say something to her?

PRIEST. No. Let us do this play first. It's essential to be frivolous sometimes. Be cheerful, General, be amusing. You're very funny in the play, do you know that? Come now, courage! Chew a bit of your red paper and go to it!
The others come in.

DOCTOR. Come along, to work, to work! On with the play! Do you know, I can't think of anything else? I rush my confinements, and when they take too long I do a Caesarian. Don't worry, the operation is perfectly safe these days. We're all here, General, when you're ready.

GENERAL (*brightly*). Off we go then, children.
To the PRIEST *as he passes.*
Was that cheerful enough?

AGLAE. Where's Monsieur Mendigales? We can't possibly do anything without our director. I wonder what's happened to him? And Monsieur Achille de Lepaud isn't here either.

GENERAL. We must get into the habit of starting on time, children, or we'll never get anywhere.
Hastily.

I mean it quite cheerfully.

> LEBELLUC *and* BELAZOR *launch into their scene.*

BELAZOR. How, sir.

LEBELLUC. Now, sir?

BELAZOR. Fie, sir!

LEBELLUC. Why, sir?

GENERAL. Quiet, you two! Let's begin at the beginning, for God's sake.

> *To* AGLAE.

The mime.

AGLAE. My dear, what can I do without Monsieur Achille de Lepaud?

GENERAL. Damn Monsieur Achille de Lepaud! First of all I allow that maggot Mendigales to put on a play here, then I let him bring his dissolute young friend Achille de Lepaud to the house, because there is nobody young enough to play Rosario—and neither of them has the decency to turn up to rehearsal! I mean it quite cheerfully. Come on then, Michepain. You start. Right then, Bise.

> BISE *and* MICHEPAIN *move onto the little stage.*

BISE. You look glum, Lucador, is anything wrong?

MICHEPAIN. I am thwarted. A woman is thwarting me.

BISE. Impossible. A gay young cavalier like you?

MICHEPAIN. There is a girl in that house opposite with whom it is impossible to deal straightforwardly.

BISE. Why not?

MICHEPAIN. She's crooked.

> *Enter* DOCTOR.

DOCTOR. What's this I hear? Don Peppino is off to the Crusades!

Enter LEBELLUC.

LEBELLUC. Is everything ready? Lucador, see our saddlebags are well stocked with meat and wine. It's a day's ride to the capital.

BISE. Madrid! Oh, how I envy you!

Enter AGLAE.

The GENERAL *goes out, escorted by the others.* AGLAE *left alone, runs to the side of the stage and calls.*

AGLAE. Rosario!

She stops.

That's Monsieur Achille de Lepaud's entrance . . .

GENERAL. Oh damn Monsieur Achille de Lepaud! You read the lines for him, Father.

AGLAE. This is where he's kissing me and we are discovered by my husband. My midnight lover!

Embarrassed, the PRIEST, *encumbered with his script, puts his arms around* AGLAE. *The* GENERAL *bursts in, in a high passion.*

GENERAL. So! The stratagem worked! You harlot! A hundred times you foiled me, but I've got you now!

He seizes the PRIEST *by the throat.*

By all the saints in Andalusia I'll . . .

SOPHIE *comes in, very upset, holding a newspaper.*

SOPHIE. Papa, I've simply got to talk to you!

GENERAL. Blast! I was just beginning to enjoy myself.

SOPHIE *collapses sobbing.*

SOPHIE. Oh, Papa! Darling little Papa!

GENERAL. Darling little Papa, eh? It must be serious! May I ask you to leave me alone with my daughter for a moment? Just do bits and pieces of the text until Monsieur Mendigales arrives.

> *They all go off, save the* GENERAL, AGLAE *and* SOPHIE, *still sobbing on the steps.*

Well, what's wrong? Tell me!

> *To* AGLAE.

Do you know what it's all about?

> AGLAE *takes the paper from* SOPHIE's *nerveless hand.*

AGLAE (*reading*). Madame and Monsieur Melchior Mendigales announce the engagement of their son Tarquin Edward Mendigales to Mademoiselle Levy-Dubois de la Rouchefoutras.

GENERAL. Bravo!

SOPHIE (*sitting up like a fury*). Papa, you're a monster!

GENERAL (*firmly*). You're unhappy, he was the love of your life, I know. But he's the third, you're twenty years old and I daresay he won't be the last. As he was an idiot I say Bravo.

SOPHIE (*hotly*). You're not to call him names!

GENERAL (*enjoying himself*). Try and stop me!

SOPHIE (*whimpering*). It was love this time, Papa! I'm sure it was love!

GENERAL. Wait until number four comes along.

SOPHIE (*sitting up, her eyes blazing*). Papa, you don't know anything about love!

GENERAL. No. Well, that is, yes—I do. A little. As much as the next man . . .

SOPHIE. You made a horrible mess of your affair with my mamma—who wasn't in love with you anyway!

GENERAL. How do you know she wasn't? Dammit, you weren't there!

SOPHIE (*going on, contemptuously*). A few casual mistresses in the odd garrison town and then you met Aglae, who's an angel of patience and resignation and who always says yes to everything. How can you know anything about a woman's heartache?

GENERAL (*exploding*). A woman's heartache! A woman's . . . ! Good God Almighty, you're my daughter and if you're not careful I'll slap your silly little face for you! Perhaps that will teach you about women's heartache!

SOPHIE. You see! That's your one stock argument—a box on the ears as if I were ten years old! Oh, my poor darling Aglae! I'm half dead with grief, but you're the one I'm really sorry for!

GENERAL (*choking*). Sorry for her! Sorry for her! And why are you sorry for her, may I ask?

SOPHIE. Because she's your wife and you don't understand the first thing about anything! Oh, what a hideous world! I might as well die now and have done with it. I'll take the veil, I'll go to Africa to nurse the lepers! I'll go on the stage!

GENERAL. I think the last solution seems most likely.

SOPHIE. That's right, your irony, your celebrated irony! Aglae, you tell him too! Tell him you're unhappy! Tell him we're

all dying of their egoism! Tell him what a man really is!
Tell him you've had enough of it too!

GENERAL (*yelling*). God Almighty, I'm the one who's had
enough. I'm sick of being accused of anything and everything every minute of the day! Was it I who announced my
engagement to Mlle. Levy-Dubois de la Rochefoutras?
    Turning to AGLAE.
Say something. You aren't saying a word and yours is the
only voice I hear.

SOPHIE (*sobbing*). I can't bear it! I can't bear it! I loved
him! I was his woman.

AGLAE. Sophie, your father's right. You'll forget him as you
forgot the other two.

SOPHIE. No, I shan't. The other two weren't up to much—
physically, I mean. I can admit it now, it was a washout.
But Tarquin Edward was my man!

GENERAL (*dazed*). The other two weren't . . .

SOPHIE (*sniffling*). No. They were hopeless.

GENERAL. But with this one you—

SOPHIE (*shrugging between her sobs*). Well, obviously. You
don't think we live our lives the way they did in your day,
do you? This isn't 1900!

GENERAL. Good God!
    He adds.
Anyway, I wasn't even born in 1900!
    Turning to AGLAE *and fighting to keep calm.*
Does she mean what I think she means or am I positively
an imbecile?

AGLAE (*with a little smile*). I think she means what you think she means.

GENERAL (*with a sudden roar*). I'll have their ears, all three of them! And the rest as well, from the last one! Wait till I get my swords!
> *He tears wildly out.*

AGLAE. My little Sophie, you've been very reckless, and very silly. And very indiscreet too. You had no right to talk about me as you did. I've never confided in you.

SOPHIE. Do you think I don't see you, clinging for grim death to your virtue? Oh, I'm paying for what I did. I'm unhappy, but I don't regret a thing. Tarquin Edward Mendigales is a self-seeking little rat, but at least I had a good time with him.

AGLAE. I love your father, Sophie, and when I married him, twelve years ago—

SOPHIE (*with sudden feminine malice*). You already enjoyed sitting by the fire and knitting socks, I know. Everyone to his taste. But even so—how can anybody be in love with Father?
> *She goes out, shrugging.* AGLAE *stands quite still, inscrutable. The* GENERAL *comes in as swiftly as he went out. He stands there for a moment, nonplused.* AGLAE *smiles.*

AGLAE. Well? Where are your swords?

GENERAL (*shrugging as he sits down*). I daresay it was absurd of me, as always.
> *A pause.*

She *was* my little girl, though. I don't know if you can

understand this, quite . . . You see, I can't get used to the idea that . . .

He stops, then murmurs.

The world doesn't turn the way it did.

AGLAE (*gently*). Yes it does. But it keeps turning, that's all. You're perched up on high somewhere and you don't understand anything about it. You must come down to our level again, Ludovic. Come, be brave! Parachute officer! Jump! You'll see how simple it all looks down below.

GENERAL (*hoarsely*). For the first time in my life, I'm afraid I might get hurt.

AGLAE (*with sudden animation*). There's Monsieur Achille de Lepaud's car! I could tell it anywhere!

> *For the first time, on hearing this name which* AGLAE *mentions so often, the* GENERAL *looks up.* AGLAE *notices and smiling, explains with complete composure.*

The sports cars those young men drive aren't exactly unobtrusive, are they? Monsieur Mendigales is sure to be with him. Now we can rehearse.

She goes out.

GENERAL (*calling after her*). Send Mendigales out to me!

> MARIE-CHRISTINE *comes hurtling in.*

MARIE-CHRISTINE. Papa! The milkman's son pinched my bottom again!

GENERAL (*giving her a steady look*). Do you enjoy it?

MARIE-CHRISTINE (*indignantly*). No, I do not!

GENERAL. Do you think girls get their bottoms pinched as often as you do if they don't enjoy it?

MARIE-CHRISTINE (*very piqued*). Very well, you have asked for this!

> *She flounces out.*

GENERAL (*yelling*). Asked for what? Great God Almighty, asked for what?

> *Enter* BISE, *breathless.*

BISE. Ludovic!

GENERAL (*barking*). Yes!!

BISE. I've just heard the dreadful news! That poor dear child's despair! The broken engagement!

GENERAL. So?

BISE. I'm afraid I may be responsible, Ludovic!

GENERAL. What—again? What for? If you think I have time to bother with your emotional states at a time like this!

BISE (*quietly*). Ludovic. I've had long talks with Monsieur Mendigales about the love of older women, their particular blend of sensuality and tenderness, and I'm afraid I may have influenced him. I'm so tired of making people suffer, Ludovic! My personality has an influence that I can't control. I bring out the worst in people.

GENERAL (*advancing on her with clenched teeth*). Don't worry, Bise. Only in me. Now get out before I strangle you.

BISE. Ludovic! I've never seen you look like this! You look positively bestial!

GENERAL (*roaring*). Go away!

> BISE *runs out with a terrified squawk.* TARQUIN EDWARD MENDIGALES *walks in very much at ease.*

Sir!

MENDIGALES. I believe you wanted to talk to me, General.

GENERAL. I do. You have, needless to say, no notion of honor?

MENDIGALES (*appearing not to have understood*). I'm rather young, as yet. But Father has the Legion of Honor to make up for it.

GENERAL (*grunting*). And you've never held anything remotely resembling a sword, I don't suppose. A foil perhaps?

MENDIGALES. No. I never took up fencing at school. I was very good at ice hockey though.

GENERAL. I see. As I have never held a hockey stick, any encounter between us, on either ground, would consequently amount to murder. Never mind. Fists were made before hockey sticks.

MENDIGALES. I don't understand.

GENERAL. You soon will. Have you seen this morning's paper?

> He hands it to him. MENDIGALES *casts a rapid glance at the offending item.*

MENDIGALES. Oh, really! Father is hopeless! I told him he wasn't to announce it yet! Has Sophie seen this?

GENERAL. She has.

MENDIGALES (*sincerely distressed*). Poor little Sophie. I wouldn't have hurt her for the world. Oh, how silly! How too silly! Father is such a child! He couldn't wait to impress his friends and show off about it at his club. I'm very sorry about this, for Sophie's sake, General.

97]

GENERAL. Young man, when they presented the Legion of Honor to your father, did they not give him a little booklet explaining the rudiments of it?

MENDIGALES. The rudiments of what?

GENERAL. Honor.

MENDIGALES (*amused*). Possibly. But Father never reads circulars, he's far too busy.

GENERAL. That's what I was afraid of. And I suppose it wasn't in the curriculum of the elegant school you no doubt went to?

MENDIGALES. I was educated in Switzerland. We learned skiing mostly.

GENERAL. Well, it's never too late to learn. You can spare five minutes, can't you? I'll give you your first lesson.

MENDIGALES. On what?

GENERAL. Honor.

MENDIGALES (*stiffening*). I need no lessons in honor from anyone, General.

GENERAL. You're proud, I see. Good. That's something to build on, anyway. You expressed sympathy for Sophie, just now. You aren't, therefore, entirely devoid of conscience?

MENDIGALES. If it weren't for Father's infantile vanity this would never have happened. That announcement should have gone in in three months' time, not now!

GENERAL. And in three months' time, what then?

MENDIGALES. I should have finished my stretch at the factory, my little affair with Sophie would have been over—for both

[98

of us: she'd have sent me a flippant little note congratulating me—as I would myself, in her case—and that would have been that. But today, I admit, it's too soon, much too soon. Believe me, General, I'm most distressed about it.

GENERAL. What's the matter with the world!
  Genuinely trying to understand him.
Look, I'll admit there's a gulf between one generation and the next; I'll willingly grant you that time and the world marches on. But dear God, we're both men, aren't we— with two arms, two legs, a belly, a heart and a brain! Members of the human race still have one or two points of contact, don't they?

MENDIGALES (*sitting down, very much at ease*). You know, General, in view of the lightning speed of technical progress these days, man is bound to reassess his fundamental problems every ten years or so. May I smoke, sir?

GENERAL. No.

MENDIGALES (*putting his cigarettes back in his pocket*). So sorry.

GENERAL (*with a touching attempt at logic*). Whether a man lights his house by pressing a switch or rubbing a tinder box, you can't tell me it makes the slightest difference to what is in his heart. Human beings have never changed, young man, and they never will. They can blow up this planet or organize it any way they like, but the real problems will remain what they have always been. You're handsome or you're ugly. You're bright or you're a fool. You've got some or you haven't.

MENDIGALES. Some what, General?

GENERAL. For the time being, let's say honor.
Wrapping his dignity around him.
Sir, you have taken advantage of my daughter.

MENDIGALES. You use some very exaggerated terms, General.

GENERAL. Is she or is she not your mistress?

MENDIGALES. There, you see? We aren't even talking the same language. Sophie and I are very good friends. I wasn't the first man she tried to share her pleasure with and I won't be the last, I'm sure. And then, one day, she'll settle down. Look at me, I'm getting married myself. We all do, for one reason or another—force of circumstances, physical attraction sometimes, lassitude quite often, mutual interest maybe, or else money. For money has never ceased to matter horribly. There I entirely agree with you—that's a notion which has altered very little with the times.

GENERAL. So you're marrying for money.

MENDIGALES. In a sense. Not that I set out with that idea. These things are never as simple as you seem to think, General. My future wife is, incidentally, a most attractive girl. She and I were very good friends too, some two or three years back. Then we parted, I forget why, quite. We met again some months ago and now we're getting married. The beauty of it is that we'll have no unpleasant discoveries. At least we know the physical side of it will work out all right.

GENERAL. But what about love? Sophie loves you! She was crying her heart out just now!

MENDIGALES (*sympathetically*). It's the shock. But she's a mature, intelligent girl, she'll take the sensible view in a day or two. You look bewildered, General. Please try to understand us. Either way, love as such is a total loss.

GENERAL. A total loss?

MENDIGALES. Of course. Your generation taught us that, with the mess you made of your personal relationships. I ask you, what choice did your generation have? On the one hand, the illicit love affair, based on vanity and embittered by tears and recriminations. Or else a so-called love match: a girl, touchingly young, with whom you leap into marriage because she smells of apple blossoms and who, two years later, turns into her own mother. In either case you hadn't a hope.

GENERAL. But, dear God, there is such a thing as real love! Otherwise, we'd all have been dead long ago.

MENDIGALES. Of course there is, but it's very rare. We wisely plan nothing with love in view, that's all. If we find it, we'll do as you do, naturally. We'll sigh and weep for as long as it lasts. We aren't rigid about this, you know. You really ought to let me smoke, General. I can't carry on any sort of discussion without smoking. It's a conditioned reflex.

GENERAL (*dazed*). A conditioned—?

MENDIGALES. You've heard of Pavlov's salivating dog, haven't you?

> MENDIGALES *lights his cigarette at last, which puts him even more at ease, if possible.*

You know, General, there is a very delicate art, faintly comparable to the art of strategy, which you really ought to cultivate a little. It's the art of living. Now you, General, are the very prototype of a man who doesn't know how to live.

GENERAL (*mesmerized*). Me—the prototype of a man who—

MENDIGALES. Of course. I won't even refer to your relationship with Aglae, which is fearfully superficial and will blow up in your face one of these days. And as for your dealings with your children . . .

GENERAL. I'm not bringing my children up right; is that what you mean?

MENDIGALES. You haven't even learned how to be a friend to them. Sophie hasn't the slightest confidence in you. And we won't even mention Marie-Christine! Toto—

GENERAL. You leave Toto alone!

MENDIGALES. Toto is your triumph, you think? You've already stuffed his head with catch phrases about honor. Believe me, it isn't lectures in Spartan severity that child needs, it's lessons in ease and flexibility. Do you think there's a future in stiffening yourself against every mortal thing in life? Come, come, General. . . .

> He stubs out his cigarette and draws out the packet.

Won't you have a cigarette? Do.

GENERAL. No.

MENDIGALES (*easily*). Relaxation, General, that's what you need. Life is fun, and it's extremely easy, in spite of what you think.

> He settles back in his chair.

You know, your whole attitude to living is so incredibly unrealistic. Take your conspiracy. Between ourselves, now, is that an adult way to carry on?

GENERAL. Conspiracy? What conspiracy? I don't follow you.

MENDIGALES (*smiling*). You even believe it's a secret. How sweet! It's the talk of the neighborhood. The authorities know all about it, but nobody takes it seriously, you know. Don't worry, they won't even put you back in prison. Do you think a dozen old men thumping the table and deploring the fact that things aren't what they used to be will make a jot of difference to the great economic realities which are shaping the world of tomorrow? Of course they won't! Why, you couldn't even influence the voting at the local elections! Don't you see that you're beaten before you start? Your love for the common people is doomed to failure because you expect too much. They tell me you bandage your gardener's varicose veins twice a week. And what's the result? Your gardener loathes you. Perhaps because of your attentions. I can assure you Papa doesn't treat his workmen's varicose veins. But he keeps them amused with co-operative meetings on factory policy and he votes as far left as they do. They built the pyramids with strokes of the lash, now they build them with union meetings and industrial talks, but nobody's fooled. Except a few eccentrics like you, who still haven't grasped the basic facts of life. The main thing is to sweat your slave, if not in one way then in another, since the world is built on his labor—and always will be, for the very reason that he makes up the vast majority. So one has to join in the pretense. It's as simple as that. Look—you haven't enough to keep you busy, that's your trouble. I could have a word with Father if you like. A general, even if he can't do much, always looks good on a board of directors—

> The GENERAL *stiffens and strikes* MENDIGALES *twice*

> *across the face.* MENDIGALES *throws away his cigarette and gives the* GENERAL *a massive punch on the jaw, which sends him sprawling among his garden chairs.*

MENDIGALES (*quietly*). General, you must excuse me, but in my elegant college, as you call it, they also taught us self-defense.
> *A short pause. He adds coldly.*
I'm very sorry, General. But I'm sure you'll understand that I couldn't just stand by and let you hit me.
> *The* GENERAL *has struggled to a sitting position. He squats on the floor, nursing his chin among his upturned chairs.*
Will you allow me to help you up, General?

GENERAL. No thanks! Go away! I'm staying on the ground! I'm thinking.
> MENDIGALES *gives a puzzled little bow and goes out. The* GENERAL *stays on the ground, thinking. The* DOCTOR, LEBELLUC, MICHEPAIN *and* BELAZOR *enter carrying benches. The* GENERAL *is still lying on the ground.*

LEBELLUC. What are you doing, General?

GENERAL. I've been thinking about the immortal words of Marshal Foch.
> *Quoting.*
"My left has crumbled, my right is shattered, my rear is in ruins, I attack." Gentlemen, these next rehearsals are in fact providential. They will enable us to meet for a few days more without arousing suspicion. The fact is, we have

been betrayed. After the play, we will make plans for going underground.

DOCTOR (*ill at ease*). Oh, General . . . I've been meaning to tell you . . .
> *Hastily.*

As far as the play is concerned, I'm with you all the way, of course. In fact, I'm seriously thinking of starting a permanent amateur Dramatic Society! Now, about the movement . . .

GENERAL. About the movement?

DOCTOR. I've given the matter a great deal of thought. To begin with, the present state of the country disturbs us all, of course, but we don't even see eye to eye on how to do anything about it. Our last discussion made that very clear.

GENERAL. Very well. I shan't be counting on you, Doctor. Come to think of it, I never did anyway, much. You have caught the spirit of the times. It's one of the rare diseases on which antibiotics have no effect. You're an honorable man, I know I don't need to recommend discretion.
> *The* DOCTOR *nods and withdraws slightly. The* GENERAL *catches* LEBELLUC'S *eye.*

LEBELLUC (*mumbling*). As for me, General . . . Well, you understand—
> *He stops.*

GENERAL (*pitilessly*). Not yet I don't. Proceed.

LEBELLUC. The ideas behind it all interest me very much. But I'm bound to say the whole enterprise strikes me as just the tiniest bit risky. To put it plainly, all we can be sure of getting out of this is a broken jaw. Suppose some hecklers break in on one of our meetings . . .

GENERAL. Well?

LEBELLUC. I'll make no bones about it, I don't like violence. I think the whole thing should be run on more democratic lines. I don't know if you take my meaning at all?

GENERAL (*grimly*). I take your meaning, Lebelluc.
> *Turning to* BELAZOR, *who is standing a little way away, visibly ill at ease.*
What about you? You've something to say to me too, unless I'm much mistaken.

BELAZOR (*embarrassed*). Well, Lulu, in my case, it's a bit different . . .

GENERAL (*coldly*). Just for now, spare me the Lulu, will you?

BELAZOR. As far as the ideas go, I'm with you, you know that. And violence doesn't scare *me*. Only . . .
> *He stops.*

GENERAL. Only? . . .
> *Relenting.*
Would you like these gentlemen to leave us while we wash the dirty linen? Gentlemen, I don't think the scenery is quite in position. Would you mind seeing to it? Then we can start rehearsing as soon as the others come down.

DOCTOR. Certainly, General. No hard feelings, I hope? We're all good men, you know, even if some small shades of opinion do divide us.

GENERAL. I know it, Doctor. But the shades of opinion that

divide good men in times of crisis are sometimes as thick as prison walls.

> LEBELLUC, MICHEPAIN *and the* DOCTOR *disappear behind the curtain. The* GENERAL *has followed them up onto the little stage. Now he turns and shouts down to* BELAZOR.

Well? Come on, out with it!

BELAZOR (*piteously*). I wish you'd come down off there. You're making me nervous.

GENERAL. Right.

> *He comes down.*

BELAZOR. Well . . . it's like this . . . You're going to think me a prize rat . . .

GENERAL. I might. Take a chance on it.

BELAZOR. You see, ideals are all very well, but life has to be lived too. And it's quite an art, living.

GENERAL. I know. I've already been told.

BELAZOR. I've specialized in what you might call the lighter aspects of it—you know me. . . . I do have a tough side, but I don't use it every day.

GENERAL. Afraid you'll wear it out?

BELAZOR (*beaming*). That's better! I was hoping you'd make a joke of it.

GENERAL (*grimly*). I am not joking.

BELAZOR (*soberly*). Well, yes. I don't use it every day so as not to wear it out. Exactly. Toughness, you see, is at a premium. It has to be kept for great occasions. I had plenty in 1940, you'll grant me that?

GENERAL. Skip the war. Let's move on to peacetime.

BELAZOR. Quite. I'm coming to that. Peacetime is when the trouble starts. Wars are easy.

GENERAL. Yes, but they don't last. Come to the point.

BELAZOR. Yes. Well now . . . my forebears, as you know, built the family stronghold at the very top of a hill. In the 15th century, from the point of view of withstanding attack, it was an exceptional position.

GENERAL. I don't see the connection.

BELAZOR. Well, give me a chance! You realize that I don't have electric light?

GENERAL. Well, if you've such an itch for progress, go ahead. Have it installed.

BELAZOR (*plaintively*). And I haven't even got running water! My wife has her bath the way her grandmother did, by heating water in Michepain's saucepans. In summer my well runs dry for want of an electric pump. I don't wash these days, I rub. And I have twenty bedrooms where you can only see your way about by candlelight. To cut a long story short, I need power, cables, a transformer, etc., etc. . . .
Wailing pitifully, but a little embarrassed too.
Seven million francs they want, to bring the cables up that hill! It's beyond any private individual's means. Especially mine.

GENERAL (*implacably*). Apply to the Council.

BELAZOR. They've been telling me to go to hell for the last twenty years and I don't blame them. Can you see yourself paying extra taxes so the Baroness can have a bath?

GENERAL. You're listed as a historical monument. Apply to the nation.

BELAZOR (*quietly*). I did. I asked it to dinner.

GENERAL. Who?

BELAZOR. The nation. Pangras. The Minister of Fine Arts.

GENERAL. You asked him to dinner! That Judas? That pseudo left-wing humbug who fiddles the nation's petty cash? That slimy lickspittle who feathers his greasy nest in the name of the working class? That stinking bag of useless wind?

BELAZOR (*pathetically*). Himself. Yes. The Baroness wined and dined him like a king. Candles on the table (that was a discreet hint for a start), her in the family jewelry, me in tails and old Julian in his threadbare livery—the whole moth-eaten paraphernalia. But it worked. After the second bottle of my oldest Chambertin, the old rhinoceros starts to reminisce about France's vanished glory. And there was I, fawning on him. Talking Socialism to right the balance (he was becoming a bit too conservative—he was starting to enthuse over the old-world charm of candlelight, it worried me). I tell you I *groveled*. I blush when I think of it. And it takes a lot to make me blush.

GENERAL (*more and more irritated*). I still don't see the connection.

BELAZOR. You aren't helping me, Lulu. I know you're an army man, but even so . . .
    A pause, then he makes a clean breast of it.
I received the notification last night. I'm getting power, cables, transformer, the lot. And as for the seven million— we foot the bill.

GENERAL. What do you mean—we?

BELAZOR (*modestly*). The nation. She's handing round the hat for me. Only, you understand . . . after that pretty little session, I shall have to look as though I hold the right opinions. Otherwise they'll cut me off.
> *A pause. The* GENERAL *says nothing.* BELAZOR *is suddenly ashamed. He sighs and says simply.*

There it is, old darling.
> *An awkward silence.*

GENERAL (*dully*). Get out, I don't want to know you.

BELAZOR (*pleading*). Lulu!

GENERAL. Painted your face, have you? Right. Go and act in the play with the others. I'll join you. After the 2nd of August, the priest will have his Charity funds, and finish. Finish to everything. You first. Forget the way to this house. Stay in your floodlit eagle's nest. I shan't disturb you. Go on! Get out! Go and take your baths! You're right, you *are* grubby. Anyone can see you haven't washed for years.

BELAZOR (*after a pause, distressed*). Ludovic . . . we've known each other since we were children. I'm the only one who cares about you. If you send me away too you'll be all alone. Oh, really, you're being too silly now!

GENERAL (*bellowing*). I should hope I am too silly. I should hope I will be all alone! Go and put your funny hat on! We start the play-acting in fifteen minutes!
> BELAZOR *opens his mouth to speak. He tries to express his regret, then abandons the attempt, goes up the steps and disappears behind the cur-*

tain. MICHEPAIN *pops his head through the curtains, wearing a heavy, clownlike make-up. He gazes with doglike devotion at the* GENERAL, *who has remained motionless at the foot of the steps.*

MICHEPAIN (*timidly*). General.

GENERAL. Yes.

MICHEPAIN. You still have me. Michepain, reporting for duty! Together we'll carry on the Movement, General.

GENERAL. Thank you, Michepain.

MICHEPAIN. It isn't numbers that count, General.

GENERAL. No.

MICHEPAIN. It's quality.

GENERAL. Yes.

MICHEPAIN (*kindly*). I know I'm all piss and wind—
　　　He makes a faint show of standing to attention.
Between soldiers, General.

GENERAL. Yes.

MICHEPAIN. But I love France, General.

GENERAL. (*suddenly weary*). I know. Stand easy, Michepain.

MICHEPAIN. And love can make up for brains.

GENERAL (*with a gleam of hope*). Do you think so, Michepain? Can it?

MICHEPAIN (*modestly*). I read that in a book.

GENERAL (*gently, suddenly discouraged*). At ease, Michepain, at ease. I'll summon you for our next meeting. Let's concentrate on the play for now. That's objective number one. We mustn't try to see too far ahead. Is everything ready?

MICHEPAIN. All present and correct, sir! We're just waiting for you and your wife.

GENERAL. Here she is. Tell the others we're just coming.

AGLAE *has come in, in full costume.* MICHEPAIN *disappears behind the curtain.*

AGLAE. We'll have to find someone to take Sophie's place right away. Thank goodness she only had a small part. She packed a suitcase and she left on the five o'clock bus.

GENERAL. Left? Left for where?

AGLAE. Brussels. Her mother is on tour there with some operetta.

GENERAL. Her mother.

AGLAE. She asked me to give you her love and to say that she was too unhappy to talk to you.

GENERAL. I see.

A pause. He adds anxiously.

Whom will she introduce her next young man to now?

AGLAE (*indifferently*). To her mother, I imagine.

GENERAL (*dully*). Yes. Poor little Sophie.

AGLAE (*softly, with a ghost of a smile*). She's not so very little. She has her own life to live now. Everyone grows up, my dear.

GENERAL. So badly, though . . .

AGLAE. Besides, don't worry, in a fortnight she'll have quarreled with her mother, and she'll come back to you. I thought we might ask Monsieur Galuchat's youngest daughter to play the part. I heard her do a recitation on last

Prize-Giving Day, and she's quite good. I called her for six o'clock. She's learning the part now.

GENERAL (*admiringly*). I see the theatre has turned you into a woman of decisions.

AGLAE. After your ridiculous scene with Tarquin Mendigales, somebody had to take things in hand.
> *She goes up on to the little stage to join the others. Then she stops and says lightly.*

As a matter of fact, Monsieur Achille de Lepaud is being a great help. I can't think why you deprived us of that young man's company for so long.

GENERAL (*grunting*). He's a young drunkard who does nothing but chase after women.

AGLAE. I think he's an extremely pleasant companion and when the play is over, I very much hope that we'll see something of him.

GENERAL. Let's do the play first. After that, we'll see.

AGLAE (*bitterly*). That's as far as this great blaze of jollity will go, isn't it? It will be your debut and your swan song, won't it? I can feel that you're hankering for your pipe and slippers.

GENERAL (*gravely*). Aglae, I would like us to devote more time to our children. Since you've been absorbed in this play, they've been left to their own devices. Toto strikes me as rather unsettled.

AGLAE. Toto is always complaining about something. He's growing like you already. My children are very happy. Besides I'll have all the time in the world to play at nursemaid when we're reduced to the company of Lebelluc and the Doctor and your beloved Belazor.

GENERAL. I have broken off relations with the Doctor.

AGLAE. That's unwise in a neighborhood as small as this. There isn't another.

GENERAL. I'll show him my bottom if I'm ill, not my face. Lebelluc is a coward and I abhor cowards. As for my beloved Belazor, he's positively off my visiting list.

AGLAE (*softly*). That leaves the priest, to give us absolution for the sins we'll never commit.

GENERAL. That leaves us, and our children. It's a great deal. It's the whole world.

AGLAE (*with a hint of malice*). They say it's a small world, don't they?

> *A pause.*

GENERAL (*gently*). We were happy once, Aglae, weren't we, you and I? You were the one who never wanted to see people. You've forgotten our long evenings, when you used to talk away for hours on end, curled up in my arms. You would stop sometimes and look up at me and say, "I talk too much, don't I?" It was you who was afraid of boring me, then.

AGLAE. I was a little girl. You seemed grown up and awe-inspiring to me. I used to think I wasn't good enough for you.

> *Lightly, as if relieved.*

How stupid one is at that age! I must have wearied you a little, admit it?

GENERAL (*huskily*). No, Aglae.

AGLAE. You say that now to please me, but I must have been such a goose, always gaping at you with admiration, afraid of my maids and afraid of the men who dared to eye me in the street. I used to run all the way home thinking I'd been violated, and take refuge in the smell of the tobacco in your study, the only place where I felt safe in the whole wide world.

GENERAL (*murmuring*). What nostalgia there is in the words, "used to be."

AGLAE. Be honest, you did prolong that state of affairs a little, didn't you, Ludovic? That is the only real reproach I have to make to you.

GENERAL. I merely left you to blossom undisturbed like a little plant that was rarer than the rest, without daring to touch you.

AGLAE (*gently*). And without opening the windows too wide either, to let the sunshine in.

GENERAL. Yes, I may have been jealous of the sunshine too. But I felt so warm and safe in our slightly somber lair, with you and our two little ones . . .
> *He says suddenly, in an odd tone of voice.*
I do believe I was in love with my family.

AGLAE. Yes.

GENERAL. I built a ring around us, and I mounted guard because I knew the measure of the world. All the animals capable of human feelings live in pairs too—and alone.

AGLAE (*quietly*). Yes, my dear, but they are animals.
> TOTO *has appeared and stands looking at them.*

TOTO. Papa?

GENERAL (*giving a start*). Yes, what is it, Toto?

TOTO. Monsieur Achille de Lepaud says will Mamma come and give him a hand. He doesn't know how to put his ruff on.

AGLAE (*suddenly alive again*). I'll come right away! Achille de Lepaud is the most scatterbrained creature you ever saw! For three days now I've been explaining which is the right and the wrong side of his ruff and he still can't put it on by himself!

> *She runs lightly up the steps and disappears behind the curtains. Her clear voice is heard off stage.*

No, no, no! Not that way! Did you ever see anyone so helpless! Now keep still and let me do it. Keep still!

> *She gives a long, silvery laugh.* TOTO *has not moved. The* GENERAL *says softly, in answer to his look.*

GENERAL. It's nothing. It's Mamma laughing.

MILKMAN. Where is he?

> MARIE-CHRISTINE *and the* MILKBOY *tiptoe in and hide behind the curtains on the little stage. The* MILKMAN *stalks in, black as thunder.*

MILKMAN. Where is he?

GENERAL. Who?

MILKMAN. My boy!

GENERAL. I don't know. I'm not his nursemaid.

MILKMAN (*fuming*). He hasn't got a nursemaid, you swine! And he can't afford to play about on Saturdays either. He's a poor man's son: Saturdays he has to work like everybody else. He's got my cart to wash down.

GENERAL. Let him wash it then. I don't give a damn what he does.

MILKMAN. Get it into your head once and for all that he isn't here to entertain the brats of the rich! We know your methods. Give the lad a bit of bread and jam and then put him to clean the boots. My boy isn't a flunky! And another thing. I won't have him learning any more of the things he's learning here!

> *Bawling.*

Look!

> *He leaps over to the stage and pulls out his son and MARIE-CHRISTINE, both as red as beetroots. He starts to belabor his son savagely with his feet and fists.*

When you've got her with child who'll pay for the brat's board and lodging, answer me that? You louse! You rat! You dirty little pig!

> MARIE-CHRISTINE *has fled, her hands over her ears.*

TOTO (*terrified*). Papa! Papa! Do something!

GENERAL (*gently*). All right, my boy.

> *He goes to the MILKMAN, tears him off his son, turns him around and hits him twice across the face. The MILKMAN gives a roar and leaps on him.*

TOTO (*claps*). Come on, Papa, knock him down!

> *A short struggle in which the GENERAL is visibly getting the worst of it. Finally the MILKMAN butts him in the stomach and sends him sprawling*

> *among the chairs, in the same spot where* MENDI-
> GALES *knocked him down.*

MILKMAN. You asked for it, you Fascist murderer!
> *He strides off, dragging his son after him. The*
> GENERAL *comes to.* TOTO *has rushed to him.*

TOTO. Papa!

GENERAL. It's nothing. I fell soft. It's familiar ground.

TOTO. Did he hurt you?

GENERAL (*grimacing slightly*). Toto, blows don't hurt. You only think they do.

TOTO (*with a sudden cry*). Papa, I'll never go and be a soldier.

GENERAL (*rising painfully*). I hope not, my boy. But you mustn't talk like that. One never knows whether one mightn't have to go and fight one day.

TOTO. I'm afraid of getting hurt.

GENERAL. You soon get used to it. There are more important things than listening to the pain one feels, Toto. Do you have any Ministafia left?

TOTO. Yes. I'm saving it up.

GENERAL. You mustn't be too sparing with it. Perhaps that's why you're frightened. Let's chew a little bit together.
> TOTO *gives him a piece of Ministafia. They chew*
> *it together solemnly, facing each other in silence.*
There. Tonight I'll call on the milkman and this time it'll be he who falls down among his milk cans. You haven't any doubts about that, Toto, I hope? Mind you, had he been a gentleman, he would have waited till I got up again

to see what I was going to do. Never mind. He'll know tonight. Now we must do some rehearsing.

TOTO. I don't want you to go! He's stronger than you are!

GENERAL (*gently*). That doesn't much matter, Toto, in spite of what you just saw. In battle, so long as you aren't dead, there's always the chance of recovery. Do you know the story of Joan of Arc and the English?

TOTO. Yes.

GENERAL. She wasn't the strongest either.

TOTO. Yes, but you're not Joan of Arc.

GENERAL (*struck by this*). True enough.
> *He adds.*

But don't forget, she wasn't Joan of Arc either, at first.

TOTO. Who was she then?

GENERAL. A little shepherd girl who couldn't do anything at all. And you see what she turned out to be!

TOTO. Yes, but God gave her a hand.

GENERAL (*quietly after a pause*). We must hope that God still will lend a hand, Toto. What on earth does Father Gregory teach you? Doesn't he tell you about God?

TOTO. No. He teaches me my catechism.

GENERAL (*with a smile*). Ah, how complicated everything is always. I'll explain it all to you when you're a big boy.
> *He looks at him and says awkwardly, with a sigh.*

Make haste, Toto. You've been little for such a long time.

TOTO (*a little wistfully*). Yes, but when I'm grown up, you'll be old.

GENERAL (*patting him on the shoulder*). We'll see if we can't meet somewhere on the road, sir.

> MICHEPAIN *appears through the curtain.*

MICHEPAIN. General, we're all here when you're ready.

GENERAL. Right! Just coming!

> MICHEPAIN *disappears.*

Now Toto, we're going to do something which is also very important. We're going to act our parts just like we do in life. In life, we must have courage, we must have our little supply of Ministafia, and we must act our parts with a smile. "Man is an animal, inconsolable and gay." I'll explain that to you too, one day. The main thing is to be able to look yourself in the face in the morning, when you shave. Here, give me another bit!

TOTO (*fumbling in his trouser pocket*). You're just gobbling it! We're wasting it!

GENERAL. Today is an exceptional day.

> He eats another piece of Ministafia, and then sits
> TOTO *on a chair with his back to the audience,*
> facing the little stage.

There. You sit there, by yourself. You'll be our audience.

TOTO. Is it a funny play? Will it make me laugh?

GENERAL. Very funny. And if at some point it isn't quite so funny, don't be scared. It's only make-believe.

TOTO. Oh, I know. I've seen a puppet show.

GENERAL. Well, Toto, you'll see when you grow up that life, even when it seems real and earnest, is still only a puppet show. And we always act the same play, too.

TOTO. But isn't it all right to laugh, then?

GENERAL. Yes. That is the engaging thing about man, Toto. He laughs regardless.

> *He dons his helmet, picks up his sword and vanishes behind the curtain. As the footlights come up, the curtain parts revealing a small replica of the show curtain. Then the large show curtain comes in, followed by the house curtain.*